GREEN

Edited by
**Austin Bowers
Lyman Missimer IV
Cyrus Akrami
Cody Kittle**

Kiva

Loans that change lives

GREEN is proud to announce that 100% of profits from sales will be used in fighting global poverty.

Kiva has facilitated more than $216 million in microfinance loans.

Profits will go to entrepreneurs through Kiva, a microfinance organization that helps alleviate poverty by connecting individual lenders with business owners in develping countries. Entrepreneurs sometimes seek out loans of as little as $100 to get their small businesses going.

For information on the business owners that GREEN is currently funding, please visit:
http://www.kiva.org/lender/greenbook

Thank you for joining GREEN's mission to help fight global poverty.

GREEN Disclaimer

GREEN is an UNOFFICIAL publication that shares no affiliation with Dartmouth College and receives no support from Dartmouth College.

GREEN is intended to be an unofficial Dartmouth student companion, written in a casual and humorous manner. It has no affiliation with the faculty, staff, or administration of Dartmouth College. GREEN is intended to be an unofficial advice book, written with a candor other College publications cannot match because of their associations, responsibilities, and liabilities. For all OFFICIAL information, see Dartmouth College's website at www.dartmouth.edu or contact the proper College representative.

The writers, editors, designers, and illustrators of this book would like to say that we are in NO WAY responsible or liable for bad ideas or actions that anyone might take because of GREEN. Many things students do at college are outrageous and imbecilic. Although we document and describe many traditions at Dartmouth, we do not recommend anything that will endanger you or anyone else. This book is written to help students enjoy their time at Dartmouth while sacrificing neither life nor limb.

Some rules that need to be established now are rules you should already know. First, don't do anything illegal! Don't drink underage, don't drink and drive, don't use illegal drugs, don't steal, and don't vandalize property! If you choose to do something illegal, it is your own responsibility to deal with the consequences. Next, don't do anything that is going to hurt you or your friends. Use alcohol responsibly. If you or your friends are ever in trouble, suck it up and tell someone in an authority position immediately. It will always be worth it. Moreover, obey College rules! If you do not, you may fail classes, be thrown out of housing, be expelled from the College, or get arrested.

Lastly, be accountable for yourself. Make the decisions you know are right and you'll always be fine. So if you think you have an idea of how to act or what to do because of this book, and this idea is illegal, dangerous, against College policies, or just downright stupid, then DON'T DO IT! If you do attempt something stupid, don't say we didn't warn you! We wrote and published GREEN to make life for students easier, happier,

GREEN Disclaimer

and healthier. Please don't do anything to make your life, or the life of others, anything contrary to our goals.

The writers, editors, designers and illustrators of GREEN would like to say that what we have written is in no way fact, nor do we claim it to be; we have written this book to provide well-intentioned advice, entertainment, and humor. Any and all information within is subject to change. The things we have documented represent our feelings toward life at Dartmouth. We have done our best to be even-handed and objective, but because of our proximity to this school (all people involved are, or were Dartmouth students) we necessarily suffer under a prejudice of subjectivity. The feelings and opinions expressed in GREEN, like any, are fallible. However, in instances when we are not being humorous or satirical, we have done our very best to report the truth. We have in no way intentionally or maliciously reported falsehoods about an individual or institution; we have in no way attempted to slander an individual or institution; and we have set out only to report our opinions and to in no way falsely indict an individual's or institution's character or integrity.

If you or any party you represent feels mistreated by this book, know that what lies within represents only the opinions of the writers, editors, designers and illustrators of GREEN. In many instances, not all of the parties involved agree with the opinions espoused in GREEN! We have expressed these opinions for the reasons stated above, and we do so with our right to free speech kept carefully in mind. Lastly, if we have misrepresented you or your interests, please contact us so that we might rectify such mistakes in subsequent publications.

All contents within this edition of GREEN are the intellectual property of Austin Bowers, Lyman Missimer and Cyrus Akrami. The content of this book may not be copied or reproduced in any form whatsoever, without the expressed written consent of Austin Bowers, Lyman Missimer or Cyrus Akrami.

Enjoy our book, be safe, and make the most of your time at Dartmouth!

Dedication

If the day you read your Dartmouth acceptance letter was one of the happiest of your life,

If a stranger becomes a friend when you discover he or she is a fellow Dartmouth student or alum,

If you swell with pride every time someone asks you where you go to school,

If you have ever referred to Hanover as "Home,"

And if you bleed GREEN,

Then this book is dedicated to you.

Acknowledgements

We would like to take this page to thank everyone who put their blood, sweat, ink, and tears into making GREEN a tangible object. With over 40 people contributing to this effort, we feel this is truly a book by students, for students. From the bottom of our hearts and souls, thank you to all contributors and readers.

We'd like to thank the brothers in our fraternities as well as the entire Greek community for their overwhelming support.

We'd like to thank Cody Kittle not only for his encouragement, but also his copy editing, without which this book would be filled with grammatical errors. We'd also like to blame him for any grammatical errors.

We'd like to thank GREEN's photographer, Kaytee Comée, and GREEN's artist, Mike Gordon, for their incredible work.

We'd like to thank Tom Mandel, Alex Black, Tyler Brace, Brendan Lane, and Bryan Giudicelli, who all went above and beyond with their contributions.

Lastly, we'd like to thank our moms and America.

Table of Contents

Introduction   11

Part I: A Dartmouth Primer
Brief History   18
Dartmouth vs. Woodward   19
Traditions   21

Part II: Preparing for Dartmouth
Checking In   32
Orientation   33
Furnishing Your Dorm   34
Miscellaneous Business   36

Part III: Student Groups
Undergraduate Societies   43
A Cappella Groups   44
Newspapers   45
Humor Publications   46

Part IV: Academics
Picking Classes   50
Academic Resources   53
Picking a Major   54
Corporate Recruiting   58
The D-Plan   60
Abroad Programs   62

Table of Contents

Part V: Freshmen Dormitories
Overviews — 68
Student Archetypes — 74
UGA: Friend or Foe? — 78

Part VI: Social Life
Hanover Police, Office of Judicial Affairs — 82
X, Pong Date, Flitzing, Dartmouth Seven — 86
Heckling Etiquette — 96
Not Going Greek? — 98
Dartmouth Outing Club — 102

Part VII: Dining
Dartmouth Dining Services — 108
Hanover Restaurants — 114
Upper Valley Dining — 126

Part VIII: Drinking
Stinson's Village Store — 132
Pong Rules — 134

Part IX: Greek Life
Overview — 148
Fraternities — 151
Sororities — 170
Co-eds — 183

Appendix — 185

GREEN
Introduction

"I prize this particular project because at least it is an eloquent gesture."

Ernest Martin Hopkins, 1945

Letter From the Editors

What is GREEN?

GREEN is the unofficial tell-all guidebook to life at Dartmouth College. Over 40 students from all corners of campus contributed to this effort, resulting in a comprehensive collection of stories, editorials, advice and perspectives. These are the kids that have been through it all and want to share their knowledge and experiences. You will learn from our mistakes and gain access to previously undocumented knowledge that will help you understand the school we have come to love.

Why GREEN?

With our time as undergrads at Dartmouth quickly fading and the "real world" only months away, we realized that we wanted to reflect on our Dartmouth experience. The College has never seen a guidebook of this candor and depth, which presented us with an opportunity to channel our experiences and nostalgia toward creating a time capsule of Dartmouth life during our time here.

We can vividly recall the anxieties that came with freshman year: moving to an entirely new place, meeting new people and trying to fit in. We get it, we really do—we also look back on our formative Dartmouth days with the understanding that we were absolutely clueless about this place when we got here. By reading this book, we cannot promise you will agree with its contents, make friends, or be any good at pong (Cyrus can attest). However, this book will provide readers with an understanding of Dartmouth and its social nuances.

For whom is GREEN?

This book is for anyone that Dartmouth has ever impacted. Whether you are an incoming freshman, prospective student, curious alum, anxious parent, or current student, this book is for you. Even after four years, we would be foolish to believe we know it all—after reading this book, you won't know it all, but at least you can pretend you do.

Who are we?

Just three good friends who don't even go here.

*Lyman, Austin, a lawn mower, and Cyrus in front of Baker

INTRODUCTION

GREEN Biases

"We hold our bias to be self-evident..."

GREEN's contributing authors come from many different social spheres and groups across campus. Naturally, one would expect a holistic representation of all campus life when these perspectives combine, right?

Maybe, but that's not what happened. **This book is biased.**

GREEN is "biased" towards Greek life, social life, fraternities, athletes, sex, and drinking. These are the ones we couldn't help but objectively notice, but surely there are more.

The point is that none of this matters.

Every student at Dartmouth has certainly sought advice from someone more knowledgeable than him or herself. This sought after advice on a particular subject is really just another word for perspective, and is undoubtedly "biased" in some way, shape, or form. GREEN is made up of each writer's perspective on the things we deem important and also care about. These 40+ writers also care about you, the reader, and **want you to be happy.**

We believe objectivity in writing is impossible, especially in the context of this book. So for your consideration, GREEN's editors have brought together as much information about Dartmouth as possible. Even if you disagree with what the authors have to say, it is still valuable to hear it.

With all that said, we sincerely hope you enjoy our 2010-2011 edition of GREEN.

Austin Bowers
>Executive Editor
>Dartmouth Class of 2011

Lyman Missimer IV
>Executive Editor
>Dartmouth Class of 2011

Cyrus Akrami
>Executive Editor
>Dartmouth Class of 2011

Cody Kittle
>Executive Editor
>Northwestern Class of 2010

I

Dartmouth *Primer*

"It is, Sir, as I have said, a small college. And yet there are those who love it."

Daniel Webster, 1818

A Brief History

Eleazar Wheelock was a very pious man

"[We] ordain, grant & constitute that there be a College erected in our said Province of New Hampshire by the name of DARTMOUTH COLLEGE, for the education & instruction of Youth of the Indian Tribes in this Land in reading, writing & all parts of Learning which shall appear necessary and expedient for civilizing and christianizing Children of Pagans..."
Dartmouth College Charter

Dartmouth began, like everything should, with fundraising. The Puritan minister Eleazar Wheelock and his first pupil, the Mohegan Native American Samson Occom, took their G-6 across America and Europe looking for sponsors for a new college (for the finance people out there, they went on a road show). During their travels, Wheelock befriended John Wentworth, Governor of New Hampshire, whose predecessor had promised 500 acres if Wheelock moved his school to his state. But Wentworth took it up a notch and offered an entire township. BAM! Wheelock established his new school in the Upper Valley as an institution for the education of Native Americans, and **on December 13, 1769, Governor Wentworth signed Wheelock's proposed charter, and Dartmouth College was born.**

Over its long history, Dartmouth has had many influential presidents, and they consistently rank somewhere between Lincoln and Polk. In the late 1800's, President William Jewett Tucker oversaw the construction of many of the College's modern day buildings and features including: thirteen dorms, the Hanover Country Club, Occom Pond, the founding of the Amos Tuck School of Business (the first graduate school of management in America, but it was less chotchy to go to back then), and the purchase of the Green. In 1945, John Sloan Dickey became president and cemented Dartmouth as a premier institution of higher learning. His commitment to the liberal arts spurred the creation of the "Great Issues" courses, foreign study programs, the Hopkins Center for the Arts, and the Tucker Foundation.

The 1970's proved to be a time of great change at Dartmouth. In 1972, **momentous change occurred when Dartmouth accepted female students for the first time in its 203-year history.** Though the decision was made amid heated controversy, the presence of females on campus has saved many Dartmouth males trips to Smith, which was essential amid recent spikes in oil prices.

Dartmouth vs. Woodward

Daniel Webster = Boss

It was in June of 1815 when the State of New Hampshire Legislature made its first strike against Dartmouth. The Legislature moved to turn the College into a public university with concentrations ranging from Hotel Management to the Agricultural Arts. However, the State could not have foreseen the irrepressible persistence with which the College would garrison its original charter.

Standing before the Supreme Court Justices, the College put forth its starting forward, its master debater, its salacious savior, Daniel "If the Charter don't fit, you must acquit" Webster. He reasoned for hours on end, not once losing the attention of the Justices. They couldn't look away, as if they were staring at a gruesome car crash on I-91... (that was a bad simile...) As if it were the first time they watched *Love Actually* (great movie).

Webster concluded his argument; he stood resolute before the entire Court for an awkwardly long time, as if to calmly stifle the fire burning in his heart. Webster stared into the eyes of Chief Justice John Marshall, and the Chief Justice leaned toward him and whispered, "Sir, Christopher Columbus with a compass would get lost in those eyes."

In the preceding moments, Webster had delivered a lucid and powerful indictment that remains the defining commentary on the relationship between Dartmouth and her faithful and loyal alumni.

Compelled by heartfelt fervor, Webster began: "This, Sir, is my case (*Oh, shit. Oh, shit*)! It is the case not merely of that humble institution; it is the case of every college in our land. It is more. It is the case of every eleemosynary (*Is that even a word?*) institution throughout our country... (*Deep breath*) Sir, you may destroy this little Institution; it is weak; it is in your hands! I know it is one of the lesser lights in the literary horizon of our country (*Shit, too self-deprecating*). You may put it out... it is, Sir, as I have said, a small College. And yet, there are those who love it (*Oh, God, I think I'm gonna boot*)—Sir, I know not how others may feel, but for myself, when I see my alma mater surrounded like Caesar in the senate house, by those reiterating stab upon stab, I would not, for this right hand, have her turn to me, and say, Et tu quo que, mi fili! (*Do they know Latin? I should translate.*) And thou too, my son!"

On the 2nd day of February in the year 1819, the United States Supreme Court, in a monumental decision, ruled that Dartmouth would remain a private institution, but I'm sure you already knew that...

Overheards   { Because **Freshmen** say the darn'dest things! }

{ "WE'VE WON TEN GAMES, LOST SIX, AND TIED TWO, SO WE HAVE HAVE AT LEAST A .597 RECORD IN BEER PONG" }

"DUDE, NO TEAM SAVES HERE!"

"WHO'S BILLY BOB?"

{ Frosh: "Hey bro, what's line like?"
AD Brother: "Uh, like 9 maybe?"
Frosh: "Oh sick, thanks, man. I'll just go f*ck myself then" }

Hungover Frosh #1: "Yo, wanna go to the Courtyard Cafe for b'fast?"
Hungover Frosh #2: "Don't they only serve coffee and pastries?"

Frosh #1: "Where are you staying for dimensions?"
Frosh #2: "Well this junior that I know said I could stay at her friend Katie E.'s House"

"IS IT COOL IF I TAKE A BEER?"

Traditions

Lest the Ol' Traditions Fail...

Few warnings could simultaneously mean so much and so little as this old adage, touted by those Dartmouth conservatives who cling to the distant past like babes prematurely weaned from their mother's teat. One becomes tempted to ask, "...or what? what will happen if the old traditions fail?" After all, the old traditions "failed" when Dartmouth started admitting women in the fall of 1972, and it forever saved the male student and local farm animal populations from many a sleepless night. Despite what grumbling alumni and Tevye from *Fiddler on the Roof* will tell you, tradition is only useful when it serves a fruitful purpose. There do exist sublimely bountiful traditions at Dartmouth, but they are so often convoluted by this misguidedly vague sense of tradition that **we forget what makes this school so traditionally fantastic: the parties.** Homecoming, Winter Carnival, and Green Key weekends are the three Musketeers of Dartmouth, provided you replace Athos with a drunken freshman, Aramus with an ice-luging professor, and Porthos with a streaking football player wearing only a bright green sock - on his foot. Together they form a triad of such wondrous revelry, **you will graduate considering Dionysus a prudish sissy-man.** In the following pages you will be given a summary of these joyous occasions, and it's of paramount importance that you read on, because there's very little chance of you remembering the real thing.

*who won the race?

Homecoming
Bonfire, Alumni, & Tomfoolery

If you open your eyes to see a multitude of pre-pubescent children running around a towering inferno, you are either within *Lord of the Flies* or experiencing the mania that is Homecoming weekend.* This is actually the **wooden conflagration that has become the iconic image symbolizing Dartmouth's first great party weekend**.

Every Homecoming is kicked off by the "running of the freshmen," which is a lot like the famous "running of the bulls," but with even more horniness and testosterone. Every freshman class traditionally runs around a colossal bonfire 100 times with their year added as an extra fitness bonus (therefore someone in the Class of 2015 will run 115 laps). Adding to the fun is that the whole school watches this spectacle and heckles in a playfully sadistic manner. For those who aren't freshmen, this is a time to relive old memories with the multitude of alumni who come up for the weekend and, in a cycle of humiliation, take out repressed memories of their freshman Homecoming out on you. **There are two specific heckles that will undoubtedly be called out to you, and it's crucial that you understand what is meant by them**. The first is "Worst Class Ever!" which is meant, of course, in jest (everyone knows the worst class ever was the Class of 1878). The second is "Touch the Fire!" which is fairly self-explanatory. What is less self-explanatory is that if you do attempt to touch the fire, you will be blindsided faster than Sandra Bullock by a burly state police officer and placed directly in jail (do not pass Dick's House, do not collect Diversions).

Unless you are a marathon runner, a weirdo, or both, **you will not finish every lap**. Instead, you will retire after around 30 to Chi Gam or Tri-Kap for one of their deliciously seedy dance parties. These parties are fun if you are single or soon to be single (a.k.a. are still delusionally dating your high school squeeze; we recommend you diversify your Portfolio). For a less sweaty time, fraternities like AD and Theta Delt are enjoyable, provided you dodge the aggressive alumni trying to relive their "glory days," which were never that glorious.

Since Homecoming is a party weekend and not just a party, it's pivotal that you learn to **pace yourself** (this holds especially true for Green Key weekend). It's a classic first-year mistake to blow one's

Fortunately if it's the latter, the only murdered Piggy you'll be receiving is when Theta Delt throws its infamous pig roast.

proverbial load on this initial night, a deleterious flub considering all Homecoming weekend has to offer. For instance, watching the football team's humiliation by the opposing school is a Homecoming experience no freshman should be without. Accordingly, at least a few freshmen will try to rush the field during the game. It should be noted that this will lead to a similar outcome as the "touch the fire" scenario, except these unlucky few will enjoy prison significantly less because they won't be inebriated.

By the time Sunday rolls around, you will get the distinct feeling that you did something stupid over the last few days, but won't know exactly what it was. Ignore this feeling, **return to your studies, and start preparing for Monday night**.

Winter Carnival

A Winter Wonderland!

In many ways Winter Carnival suffers the conventional pains of being a middle child: cold, misunderstood, lacking the novelty of being first born, but without the verdant vivaciousness of being the youngest. Still, in its own way, **Winter Carnival may be the most special of the three big weekends.** No event symbolizes Dartmouth's spirit of unique individuality more than this snow filled extravaganza. If a flaming tower of wood is the symbol for Homecoming, the famous Dartmouth snow sculpture is the symbol for Winter Carnival. Every year, Dartmouth gathers its greatest artisans, craftsmen, and snow enthusiasts to create a giant ice behemoth that is virtually indiscernible from a snowball built by Roald Dahl's B.F.G. Dartmouth is a school full of talented artists, but for an indesplicable reason not a single one can design an innovative or well constructed snow sculpture.

Despite our Ivy League pedigrees, you'll find that snow constructed into a large shapeless blob excites everyone. **The energy surrounding Winter Carnival is infectious**, if only for the reason that it's a short respite from the cold dark of winter. From winter vacation until Carnival, Dartmouth students make the slow transition from cave dwelling troglodytes into party loving sex-fiends. By the time Winter Carnival rolls along, you'll be as pale as Boo Radley dipped in almond milk. Don't be discouraged by this though; the boy/girl you've had your eye on will be equally pale and a quick swig of bourbon will soon bring color to both of your cheeks.

In terms of activities, Winter Carnival provides a cornucopia of events. For those that dabble in masochism, the **Polar Bear Swim** provides a plethora of pain-induced pleasure. In front of voyeuristic hordes, you can strip down to your skivvies and dive into the icy-cold waters of Occom Pond. Though you may find yourself resembling Jack Nicholson at the end of *The Shining*, you'll win the respect of countless onlookers (though males should note that they will be naked and the water is incredibly cold). For a temporary vacation from the frosty realities of Dartmouth, you can inspect **SAE's annual Beach Party**, which features beach balls, canopies, and even imported sand. Of course if you really crave warm weather this much, you can just book a flight to Miami and get all of those things without having to be around SAE's. One of the most exciting draws of Winter Carnival is Saturday's **Dartmouth ski race.** Though many have forgotten, Carnival was originally centered on this race and it served as a "Homecoming" of sorts for the ski team. If you've got friends on the ski team, are a speed junkie, or have a pole fetish, this race is not to be missed.

Despite these events, the reality of Carnival traditions is that, like Peloponnesian War veterans, the vast majority of them are dead. If you were to walk into your nearest old age home and find a Dartmouth alum from the Class of 1940, he would tell you of all the Carnival traditions that have gone the way of the dodo. For instance, the "Carnival Queen" in all its sexist glory, is now a forgotten vestige of the all-male campus. Every year, hundreds of college and high school girls were literally bussed to Dartmouth from all over the country in a great migration of sorts. Eventually, the least prim and proper of these drunken ladies would be chosen as "Carnival Queen". Today, the only carnival queens you'll find are up the street at Tabard, but in an admirable cycle, most girls today show no primness whatsoever.

Another discarded tradition is the Psi U Keg Jump, a show of athletic prowess in which a Psi U brother on ice skates attempts to jump and clear as many consecutive kegs as possible. The practice was eventually outlawed due to severe injury and the unmasking of a Class Dean's tupeé. It would take far too long to list all the old Carnival traditions, but one event has perhaps immortalized the weekend more than any other. In 1939, F. Scott Fitzgerald (*The Great Gatsby*) and Budd Schulberg (*On the Waterfront*) came to Winter Carnival to work on a screenplay about Dartmouth Winter Carnival called... *Winter Carnival*. The weekend ended up being both a failure and a success as Fitzgerald wasn't able to write anything but got absolutely plastered in the process. Every year students honor this event by getting incredibly drunk and failing to hand in their assignments on Monday.

Green Key

"For No Reason"

Traditionally, spring has been portrayed in music and art as lush and virginal. Dartmouth is quite lush during this period but it's very unlikely that you or your friends will be virginal by the time Green Key comes around. As a class, the seniors will be in full-on heat, but remember: don't get in a car alone with one of them, even if they offer you candy. You'll find spring seniors are desperate and lonely creatures and should be treated with extreme caution at all times. Of course, it's not only the seniors who will have unfulfilled conquests on the mind, everyone, including yourself, will want to go out with a bang before the summer starts. Because Green Key is such a busy affair, it's often helpful to go into it with some goals, a social checklist of sorts. For instance, it could read: do one of the Dartmouth Seven, do one of the Dartmouth Seven with someone else, steal one of the president's children. This will undoubtedly provide some direction to your deviance and expand the scope of the weekend's debauchery. And **make no mistake, there will be debauchery,** the kind of debauchery that produces memories you can store away, as a chipmunk does with acorns for those years ahead when you slave away in a desolate cubicle.

Though Green Key-sized parties start on Wednesday night, **the weekend really kicks off with Phi Delt's Block Party** on Friday afternoon. If someone recounts to you a detailed description of past Block Parties they are lying and possibly trying to sell you something. No one can truly say what happens on the front porch of Phi Delt every Green Key because no one really remembers. The best a Block Party veteran can tell you is that there were scantily dressed teenagers, music, and the mingling aromas of grilled food, summer air, and alcohol-infused vomit. Perhaps most importantly, the Block Party shows once again that a successful Green Keyer must take a page from the tortoise's book rather than the hare's. If you aren't slow and steady, you will not only lose the race, but also all bodily functions (the story of the kid who spent all of Green Key in a kiddie pool of his/her own urine is only amusing if it isn't you). Again, the Friday of Green Key is a trap designed to sink all newcomers into the party-ending sands of a hangover. Treat the Block Party like you would a prostitute or gigalo: have your fun but protect yourself for the future.

Saturday morning provides one of the most fun events of the weekend: the Theta Delt Pig Roast. Whoever says Ivy League students aren't vicious predators never set foot in this smoky porkfest where voracious carnivores and failed vegetarians fight each other for a handful of slow-cooked pig and warm, buttery rolls. If you are lucky enough to actually get your hands on some pig, make sure to rub it in the face of those who haven't, or couldn't for religious reasons. You'll find the barbaric joys of having piping hot pig meat in your hands eradicates the trivial "virtues" of loyalty and morality. Friendships have been made and broken over an ounce of this delicious smoked animal, and those who do get a small taste are inevitably reduced to Gollum-like creatures, pathetically waiting until the next year to have another juicy piece.

Finally, **the last great event of Green Key weekend is the Lawn Party at AD**. Excluding certain political events, this is undoubtedly the most chaos to ever happen on a grassy knoll. Every Saturday of Green Key, hundreds of students rage on the lawn outside of Alpha Delta fraternity whilst drinking beers, eating barbecue, and listening to the band that AD paid thousands of dollars to have play. Past bands have included Bang Camaro, Filligar, and Otis Day and the Knights (of Animal House fame). The Lawn Party is by far the greatest event of Green Key unless, of course, it rains. If it does rain, however, sack up and let yourself get doused (under no circumstances should you bring an umbrella). An insider's note: don't forget to actually go inside Alpha Delta during the Lawn Party. While most people will stay outside the entire time, the wise man goes into Alpha Delta and steals beer. **That's Green Key for you, in all its verdant charm... so eat, drink, and be merry!**

*some solid R&R on the AD lawn

Yea, You're in College...
but that doesn't mean you have to...

...wear your sports gear everywhere.

Dartmouth is a small school, so facetime (see appendix) is plentiful. By our calculations, just by walking from Silsby to Food Court in between 12's and 2's, you will see at least 7 people you know, 15 people you don't know, 8 people you will know, and 21 people you have no intention of talking to. After doing the math, the editors have determined that you will see more people you have no intention of talking to than any other type, and what better way to signal to those haters you are better than them than by gloating about your varsity sport status. News Flash: no one cares what team you play for (barring Men's Soccer).* Chances are extremely high you have a losing record anyway. So for the ~831 varsity athletes and roughly 208 incoming freshmen athletes: express yourself, but not by being a douchebag.

...play Frisbee.

Let's face it—nobody likes Frisbee. You either love it or hate it. If you love it, chances are that you really annoy those of us who hate it. When you ask us, "hey, brah, want to go toss a disc around?" we decline as politely as possible, but in our heads we are thinking, "I'm not a goddamn Golden Retriever." On warm sunny days, hundreds of students spend hours tossin' the disc around on the Green. If you feel inclined to participate, we suggest you try this first: think of one activity. It can be anything—catching up on emails, playing a real sport, or even shoplifting from DDS. Have something in mind? Excellent. We promise that this activity will be more worthwhile than Frisbee. For those of you thinking, "What about Ultimate? That's cool, right?" It sure is! And I'm dating Jessica Alba.

*DISCLAIMER: two of the Green editors were on the soccer team

...do everything.

The hardest part about college is getting in, or so they say. You were accepted to one of the top academic institutions in the country, but Dartmouth is more than just reading, research, and rounding up your GPA. Dartmouth will also be the source of some of the most ridiculously fun times of your life. This can and should be the case for every undergrad if they let themselves take advantage of all Dartmouth has to offer. It's physically impossible and mentally debilitating to do every reading for every class, join every 'interesting' club, and attend every performance at The Hop during your four-year career. Accept that as fact, go out on the weekends, and have some fun. You earned it.

*Dartmouth Hall on a snowy day

II

Preparing for *Dartmouth*

"Back to school, back to school, to prove to Dad I'm not a fool."

John Sloan Dickey, 2002 "Overheards"

Checking In

Tips on making your first days easier

It's Check-in Day at Dartmouth. You haven't been this excited since you were six years-old, and it was Christmas morning; you may have even peed yourself a little bit. Here are five helpful tips that will make check-in a little less stressful:

1. **Breathe** – We know you are excited, but you already got in, so chill out a little. You don't want to seem like the kid who is super eager to finally be at college (see pg. 75); no one liked the eager kid in high school and it's even worse in college. Take two seconds, realize that you made it and that you have four years to take in all the sights.

2. **Arrive Early** – Preferably even the day before. Check-In Day is actually pretty frantic with all the tents and events that have been planned. It will be infinitely better for you if you have a sense of where your room is on campus, where the Green is, etc.

3. **Enlist Labor** – Parents, siblings, high school girlfriends (just kidding), paid labor, that guy from Seattle you met, literally whoever is willing to help you move your stuff. You are moving your whole life to Hanover, which will inevitably take up more than two boxes, so having a small army of people to help is nice. Just realize that having a separate box for your stuffed animals might not be the coolest move.

4. **Diversify** – **Dad, bagels from Dirt Cowboy. Siblings, unpack clothes from boxes. Mom, decorate and put things away** ('How do you always fold things so well?!'). The tent is a huge mess, and now is the time to work on valuable delegation. Give everyone a different job, so you don't get stuck doing everything.

5. **Meet People** – #3 and #4 are important because you should be spending your time meeting people. Meet people on your floor, you will be living with them for the next year. Go out to the Green and meet people. You don't have any schoolwork yet, the weather is nice, and everyone (upperclassmen included) is happy to be back at Dartmouth. So be social, and enjoy.

Orientation
Events to actually attend

Believe it or not, you don't actually HAVE to go to any event during Orientation, but the editors recommend going to these gems:

Convocation
This is the first time you get to sing the alma-mater with your class and is another valuable chance to meet new people.

Matriculation
You should probably matriculate...

Dinner on the President's Lawn
This is a chance to shake the president's hand (probably for the only time) and again meet more possible friends. Do not attend with your freshman floor. You will get stuck with them the whole time and chances are you won't look any cooler. Bring one friend or partner in crime and meet as many new people as possible.

*the President's House

Side note:
Always come back for Orientation week after freshman year. The weather is nice, you get an objective perspective on the freshman chaos, everyone is "excited" to see everyone, and moral flexibility is at an unprecedented high (interpret as you will).

Furnishing Your Dorm
Does the carpet match the shades?

Getting Your Stuff to School

The best way to transport all the things you need and all the things you think you need to school is by driving. Unfortunately, we know (from experience) that driving is not an option for everyone. **For those who are flying, West Lebanon has plenty of options for purchasing amenities, including a K-Mart and a Walmart.** For this trip, you will need a car, as the Advanced Transit bus system is just plain inconvenient and smells like a senior citizen after a pill-box binge. Be wary though, **you cannot buy everything at Bed, Bath, and Beyond**. Here's why: it doesn't exist (at least not nearby). One final option is to order things you cannot carry on the plane online to your Hinman box, which is a surprisingly convenient and seldom-used method.

For those who are driving, **renting a Uhaul** is definitely an option; there is a U-HAUL store in close by Lebanon for dropping off the truck.

Music

All of your music from high school sucks, and no one cares how "good your taste is". **Dartmouth's underground music scene is second only to Juilliard's.*** Songs get popular here way before the radio tells you what to like. Study up on these popular music blogs before getting to Hanover.

Big Green Beats – Started by one of Dartmouth's very own, BGB brings us the best new jams, leaks, and mix-tape bangers. They have shifted towards posting the tunes of fresh up and coming artists. Although only a few years old, BGB's reputation has skyrocketed nation-wide.

Fresh New Tracks – New England's preeminent music blog, FNT features all genres of music ranging from techno to indie rock. They can always be relied upon to post the newest hits and the best underground music, as well as the odd viral YouTube video.

Crizzadizzle – Another blog started by one of Dartmouth's current students, Crizza focuses mainly on electro music and tunes to smoke to.

*citation needed

Fridge

You need one to house your beer (for those over 21, of course), carrot sticks, and drunken munchies. You can buy one yourself, or avoid the logistical nightmare of splitting one with your roommate by **using Evolving Vox, Dartmouth's most trusted dorm furnishing company.**

*an actual Dartmouth room: note the solid feng shui

Furniture

Although buying furniture is certainly a viable option for making your dorm room just like home, the chaotic nature of the D-Plan (see pg. 60) makes transporting and storing your couches, chairs, and lamps a real headache. Luckily, there is a viable and smart alternative to this problem: **Evolving Vox**. Evolving Vox is Dartmouth's oldest and most trusted student-run furnishing company. They specialize in futons (metal or wood), but also provide the Dartmouth student body with full beds (hey, couples!), mini fridges, lamps, tables, DVD players, and outdated televisions. Their service is top notch, and so are the guys who run it. Girls have been known to stand outside their dorms and giggle on those hot and sweaty delivery days, hoping to get a peek at the owners delivering the heavy furniture – topless.

Miscellaneous Business

Money

Small-town Hanover has a dearth banks to handle your finances. The most popularly used bank is **Bank of America**, and out of convenience **we recommend opening an account.** The other national bank present on Main Street is **Citizen's**, which is a convenient local option. For the more financially savvy in-comers, **Ledyard Advisors** is also available for those looking to open a 401k or diversify their portfolio. GREEN suggests avoiding the Hanover Bucks option, as we assume this will go under before this book is published (GREEN's equity analysts maintain a "sell" rating).

Communication

Cell phone-wise, Verizon has the best coverage across campus. Sprint sucks. Also, don't expect to have good service if you are in the River (Connecticut or Dorm). Cell phone use has become prominent on campus only in the last five years and has given birth to terms such as "text game" and "sexting". This is why email, specifically BlitzMail, remains a prominent medium of communication, especially in the dating/hook-up scene (see pg. 90).

Buying Books

Max Weber would be rattling the bars of his Iron Cage in rage if he encountered the bureaucratic system in place for buying books at Dartmouth. However, you really have a limited number of options, besides not buying them altogether.

Wheelock Books

Holding the title as **Dartmouth's preeminent bookstore**, Wheelock Books literally stands as the main destination for bookworms looking to buy their figurative apples. Professors place their book orders here and depending on the class, the books run out fast, so we highly suggest channeling your inner nerd and hitting up the book-"stork" as early as possible.

Top 10 Ways to Get Fined

1. Public (masterb, fornic, urin, intoxic) - ation

2. Forgetting to check in online ($50)

3. Registering your car with the College (idiots)

4. Filing your D-Plan late ($500 fine)

5. Overdue Jones and Baker rentals

6. Other people breaking shit on your floor

7. Getting Good Sammed (~$100)

8. Getting picked up by H-Po (Diversions=$400)

9. Caught on roof of fraternity / sorority ($100)

10. DDS ($1400)

PREPARATIONS

III

Dartmouth
Student Groups

"If you can't beat 'em, join 'em."

Benedict Arnold, 1774

Student Groups

Tragedy of the Commons

Dartmouth has somewhere in the neighborhood of ~75,000 student groups. There is something for everyone: World Affairs, Libertarianism, Young Engineers, Classical Ballet, Guacamole Tasting – honestly, whatever weird fetish you have, Dartmouth has a group for it. Fortunately, all of these groups are exactly the same. They meet every week, they order the same awful Chinese food or pizza (see pg. 117), and they rarely get anything done.

Dartmouth Tae Kwon Do

The best representation of student group inefficiency: Dartmouth Tae Kwon Do. Feel free to apply this review to any student group you are thinking about joining. With Dartmouth TKD, the joke writes itself. I accidentally walked into a Dartmouth TKD practice, and within five minutes had to leave out of sheer embarrassment. It was like the scene from *Meet The Parents* when Ben Stiller unnecessarily spikes the volleyball into his future sister-in-law's nose; watching it forces you to turn away in discomfort. Eight of the least athletic people I have ever seen were facing their "sensei" a.k.a. the unbelievably awkward, unquestionably fragile girl who looked like she could be defeated by a well-timed sneeze.

Beyond the fact that everyone's belts were tied like shoelaces, the actual "tae kwon do" that was taking place was comical. If you have ever taken a martial arts class, you know that the first rule is to "keep your guard up". I think there is a rule in Dartmouth TKD that if anyone moves, including the instructor, you have to keep your arms at your side like a velociraptor. Keep sweeping the leg...

Greek Leadership Council (GLC)

The Greek Leadership Council. The gathering of every president from every Greek Letter Organization on campus. It's the Boardroom. It's the War Room. It's where campus leaders gather to discuss campus issues, but don't actually do anything in the name of political correctness or bureaucratic infighting.

The GLC consists of the presidents of every fraternity, sorority, minority, and co-ed house on campus, the presidents of the Panhellenic

Council and the Inter-Fraternity Council, and the GLC executive board. These people matter. Right? Kind of? Well, they think they do, and that may be part of the problem. Everyone is always terrified of being considered politically insensitive, so campus issues are never actually discussed. But in case you would like to discuss something of the utmost importance, like if your house needs some money for a water slide, the GLC has a giant discretionary account that can help you out.

Inter-Fraternity Council "IFC"

The IFC represents and governs Dartmouth's fifteen fraternities. It is composed of the President of each house, a seven member executive board and is led by the IFC President. The IFC manages relations between the fraternity system and the administration, town, other campus groups, and between fraternities themselves. A fan would probably say that the IFC is the only major student organization with any real power that is truly independent from outside control. The IFC has been central to helping the Greek system as a whole deal with threats to its existence for many years.

Panhellenic Council "PanHell"

PanHell is the sorority system's equivalent to the IFC and is responsible for representing and governing Dartmouth's eight sororities. However, unlike the IFC, there is a much clearer distinction between PanHell as an organization and the sorority system in general. While the fraternities are pretty much governed by the same rules, and therefore have similar interests, the national and local sororities often have different sets of rules that help shape their own interests. Among other restrictions, Dartmouth's five national sororities cannot have alcoholic social events on their property, whereas the three local ones can. As a result, the local sororities have to deal with a whole host of issues stemming from the ability to throw parties with alcohol that don't affect the nationals to the same extent. Its most important job seems to be managing the sorority system's notoriously complicated, lengthy, and unpopular rush process that many girls find absolutely miserable (see pg. 172).

Programming Board

Programming Board is a student-run organization that puts on various social events around campus. These events range from concerts to movie nights. While some of these events are unbelievably dorky, I am sure there are people who enjoy tie-dying t-shirts so more (flower) power to you. During my first three years here, there seemed to be a lull in the acts that came to perform at Dartmouth, but over the last twelve months, I've actually been somewhat impressed. PB has gotten Chiddy Bang, Ke$ha, Talib Kweli, and Immortal Technique to perform. Being so far North, it is quite a difficult task to get big names to rock out in Leverone, so keep doing what you're doing Programming Board. I see you.

Sexperts

I get it! You are experts at sex...outrageous. The Dartmouth Sexperts are a campus educational group created for the purpose of "peer education around issues of healthy sexuality, **pleasure-based** sexuality, STIs, and contraception" (emphasis added, intentionally). This is awesome. Trust me, there are things you didn't learn about in High School Health. I went to a Sexperts event and I received free condoms, played with a large dildo, and participated in a blind taste testing of different lubrications! It's time everyone became comfortable with their sexuality. Sexperts, thank you for helping with that.

Student Assembly (SA)

SA is technically the representative organization of the entire student body at Dartmouth, although its main constituency is probably itself. With a few exceptions, every SA committee (there are a lot of them) draws from the same pool of idealistic/super-ambitious go-getters looking to make a difference/build a résumé.

It's not all bad, though. SA has done a great job recently promoting student safety and a responsible IFC alcohol policy. There are services SA can and should do well, such as making sure there are staples by the printers, keeping the Course Guide up, and organizing buses to NYC over Thanksgiving break. If SA would stick to this, they'd be great. Unfortunately, the countless committees that do nothing, attempt to save the world, and constantly bicker over obscure bylaws detract from its relevance to the average student.

Undergraduate Societies
Panarchy and Amarna

Panarchy

Panarchy is one of Dartmouth's four co-ed houses, a distinction that automatically ensures its status as, you know, "alternative". Originally founded in 1896 as Phi Kappa Psi, the fraternity broke from their national organization in 1967 over issues surrounding racial discrimination. The resultant local frat, Phi Sigma Psi, quickly became a haven for diversity, irony, and copious drug use. Legend has it that Phi Sigma Psi went co-ed the day women were first admitted to Dartmouth.

Today, Panarchy's men and women, better known as "manarchists" and "vaganarchists" respectively, live together in glorious, if somewhat pretentious, harmony. Despite having lost some ground to The Man in recent years, Panarchy is still one of the few houses left on campus where meetings are open to the public and binge drinking is almost weird.

A fan of the house will emphasize their commitment to diversity, the arts, and being "seriously chill". In addition, the two parties hosted by Panarchy – Rave and Gatsby – are highlights of every Dartmouth term, no matter how many steaky dudes try to hijack the scene.

A hater will remind you that techno and jazz are actually sort of shitty, that all hipsters must die, and that drugs are bad for you.

Amarna

Amarna is the short period in Egyptian history ruled over by the Pharaoh Akhenaton. He was known for his ruthlessness and eccentricity, and no one knows whether he was a man or a woman. This was arguably the first monotheistic religion to ever exist, as he declared supreme rule for the Sun God. This period was short lived though, as the noble priesthood in Egypt restored their anamorphic pantheon and their capitol city.

In all seriousness, Amarna is actually an undergraduate society independent of the Greek system, and they occupy a pretty unique niche on campus. Their official website states that members embrace diversity and scorn discrimination, and rightfully so (yay, holism). Highlights in this society's operation include their Monday Night Dinners and the termly "Wine and Cheese" parties, which are to die for! If you don't go to at least one of these events in your four short years here… go to one when you come back to visit…

A Cappella Groups

Vox Clamantis

All-Male

The **Dartmouth Aires**, founded in 1946, are the College's oldest a cappella group. Upon entry into the group, all members are given two syllable nicknames ending in "o," and are exclusively referred by these super cool names. Group members get a bad rep for being full of themselves, though they would probably sing you something to refute that.

As their name might suggest, the **Cords** wear more corduroy than well, Corduroy. The Cords have created an original and entertaining act, fusing music spanning all genres including rock, pop, hip-hop, and some College favorites. The Cords have performed in numerous locales, including the Lincoln Center. Our particular favorite is their rendition of "Uncle John's Band" by the Grateful Dead (we're total deadheads!).

Dartmouth's other all-male a cappella groups include the **Brovertones** and **Taal**.

Co-ed

The **Dodecs** are the College's premier co-ed group, with some phenomenal soloists, often with a background in musical theater. Fun Fact: the Dodecs were the first a cappella group at Dartmouth to be recognized on "Best of College A Cappella".

Other co-ed groups include the **Sing Dynasty**, and **Xado**, the College's Christian group.

All-Female

The **Decibelles** are Dartmouth's oldest all-female a cappella performance group. They are literally as old as an all-female group can get, as they were formed during the second year of co-education. Oddly enough, a small group of men have been known to masquerade around as The Decibelles, calling themselves the "Terribelles"...

The **Rockapellas** perform regularly around campus and retain a particular interest in freedom/social justice topics for their performances. The last all-female group is the **Subtleties**, who focus on innovative choreography, as well as new and interesting sounds.

Newspapers
Muckraker's Anonymous

The Dartmouth

Commonly referred to as 'The D" (ha ha... grow up), The Dartmouth is the campus' daily newspaper as well as the oldest college newspaper in the country (chew on that, Yale). Founded in 1799, it boasts a staff of more than 150 students, making it one of the largest and most visible organizations on campus.

The paper is published daily during the fall, winter and spring terms, and twice a week during the summer, and it includes weekly supplements covering Sports and Dartmouth Culture. The most-read section is Friday's Mirror, whose writers take on a different aspect of Dartmouth culture each week. And, although complaints arise fairly often (particularly from the Review and from outspoken Dartmouth Alumni that lose Trustee elections) that The D is closely connected with the College Administration, it operates under the non-profit corporation The Dartmouth, Inc., and is completely independent from the College.

The Dartmouth Review

The Dartmouth Review was founded in controversy, and it has stayed there ever since. Started in 1980 by four disaffected students who wanted to preserve old-school Dartmouth and add a conservative counterweight to the campus' liberal atmosphere, the paper quickly grew to have an outsized reputation.

This publication has long been a campus lightning rod. It continues to use the Indian mascot symbol, referring in its pages to Dartmouth sports teams as the 'Indians' and handing out free Indian head t-shirts to incoming freshmen at its yearly Orientation open house. The makeup of the paper's staff is eclectic; editorial meetings play host to a bizarre mix of frat bros, awkward freshmen, campus misanthropes and recluses, and the occasional girl. Alums from the past decade have been found clerking on the Supreme Court for Justice Samuel Alito, writing speeches for General David Petraeus, and winning the Pulitzer Prize for Editorial Writing.

Humor Publications
Ha! You thought YOU were funny...

The Dunyun

Everybody loves synergy. And that's what The Dunyun is. It took Dartmouth and The Onion, put them together, and made the spelling phonetic. Since its founding, The Dunyun has established itself as one of the pre-eminent sources of humor on this campus. Sign up to receive The Daily Dunyun to get a message each day in your inbox that makes fun of campus icons, silly administrators, the PC Police, Dartmouth athletics, freshmen, and Hanover Police, to name a few. Or check it out online at www.thedunyun.com. The authors of The Dunyun are technically anonymous, but don't let the fake facetime or the fake news fool you. It's all real.

Generic Good Morning Message (GGMM)

As if Dartmouth needed more humor publications, the daily "Generic Good Morning Message" blitz has stepped in to save the day. Each "morning" (if the authors remember), the GGMM sends a satire blitz to their exclusive blitz list, which usually entails a main section, news of the day, a haiku, weather, scoreboards, and their douche... I mean, mail, yeah mailbag.

Jack-O-Lantern

The Jack-O-Latern is Dartmouth's most-esteemed (only), award-winning (citation needed) humor magazine. The Jack-O website describes their magazine as "self-quarterly," but in all honesty, who knows? They are most well known for their paraody of The D, which is impressively funny at times. Next time you get a chance, youtube "Drinking Time"; it's the Jack-O's most famous prank.

10 Things to Leave at Home

1. Prep school memorabilia (Exeter? Don't.)

2. Your sleeveless workout shirts

3. Your pictures of high school friends

4. Your entitlement

5. Your letterman jacket

6. Your high school significant other

7. Your pet (unless it's Chia)

8. Your morals/standards/closed mind

9. Your North Face (spare us the lost jacket blitz)

10. Your "sick" high school stories

IV

Academics

"Dartmouth may not do it first, but we'll do it second - and better."

Dean Craven Laycock, 1922

Picking Classes

You have ~36 chances

If you're set on being a pre-med double major, then stop reading now. For everybody else, we have these wonderful things called "electives". That basically means that sometimes you can take whatever the f*ck you want. Freshman fall is one of these times. Use it wisely.

The most important consideration when planning out your schedule is timing. Thinking about taking that 9L that uses every x-hour? Psh. Not even. Look out for that 11 that you get out of ten minutes early each class. Beat that lunch rush hour with ease.

Timeslots to aim for:
10, 11, 12, 2A

Timeslots to avoid:
2, 10A, 9L, 9S, 3A, 3B

After you've picked the right timeslots, start looking at the kids that are going to be in the class. This is where median grades come in. You can go online and find the median grade for every class that's been taught in recent memory. For those of you who aren't too good with math, the median grade is the grade that the kid in the 50th percentile got. Half the class got that grade or higher, and half the class got that grade or lower. If you're sitting in a median A class and realize that you're probably smarter than every other person in the room, then you can rest easy. If you look around in a median B class and everybody's a senior major and definitely smarter than you, then get out. Leave. Dropping classes in college is that easy.

After this, there are things to consider, like the professor and the material. These are pretty important too, but in very specific ways.

Professor:

Pick cool professors. And by that, I don't mean, "Pick good professors." I mean, "Pick cool professors." Pick professors that you'd want to see out at a bar. Pick professors that you'd want to spark up a joint with. Pick somebody that you can listen to talk for hours without losing focus. Don't pick people based on their credentials. Some of the most qualified professors are the worst lecturers.

On the first day, if you hear the professor ask you if you think that the Japanese internment camps "were ethically permissible or if they were f*cking bullshit," then you've hit the jackpot. Major in that department. If the prof starts speaking in French during your History class, drop that shit like it's hot.

Material:

Use your judgment on this. You like what you like.

Balance of Schedule:

This is what really ties it all together. Once you've picked some cool timeslots, some lofty medians, some lazy classmates, some baller profs, and some fresh material, you have to make sure it all fits together. Taking three hard major classes? Nah. Throw an easy class (gut) in there. Taking only humanities classes? Good luck finishing your reading before 3 a.m. Add something science-y in there. Only lecture classes? By the end of the term you'll start feeling like nobody pays attention to you. Get something small in there to balance things out. All about balance.

If you ever get stuck, go online and look at SA's Course Guide. There are anonymous student reviews from the past ten years. This will tell you more about a class than anything else.

*McNutt Hall: home to the most annoying place on campus: the Registrar

ACADEMICS

Rules of Library Etiquette

Know your R.O.L.E.

Thou shalt not obnoxiously reserve seats overnight.

Thou shalt not put books and backpacks on the swivel comfy chairs to reserve them. Rude.

If you are gone from a study spot for more than three hours, fair game to have your stuff moved (The clock is ticking...).

Cell Phone conversations on 2FB and up are NOT OK.

Working in an unreserved study room? It is kosher for someone else to check, see that it's not reserved, book it, then kick you out.

If it's yellow, let it mellow; if it's brown flush it down.

One book and a pencil is not sufficient to save a spot. Nice try.

No excuses, play like a champion.

All's fair in love, war, and finals.

Academic Resources

You are not alone

Office Hours

While the academic transition to Dartmouth may seem daunting at first, know that you have access to an array of tools to help you through that seemingly 'impossible' class. With these ten-week terms, it is easy to find yourself caught in a wave of exams, papers, and presentations. The first lines of defense are your professors. **Office hours,** or the two times during the week that professors open their doors to catch up with students, **present great opportunities to voice your concerns with your professors and solicit advice from the ones dishing out the work**. They won't bite.

R.W.I.T.

The Student Center for Research, Writing, and Information Technology, or RWIT, is a great resource for Dartmouth students. RWIT is a free service provided to all members of the Dartmouth community to help create and edit papers and presentations. Located on First Floor Berry, **RWIT tutors will help you generate ideas and edit papers for your classes**. Students can easily make appointments with tutors online, and go in for help.

ASC / Tutoring

The Academic Skills Center (ASC) is a resource center whose goal is to aid students in academic achievement. Students can go to the ASC for any sort of academic need from **setting up peer tutoring sessions to seeking help in test taking situations**. The Tutor Clearinghouse pairs students with student tutors who have demonstrated skill in various subject areas. Becoming a tutor is easy: as long as you received an A or A- in the subject and are willing to work three hours a week, you meet the requirements and will earn $9/hour.

Picking a Major

Do what interests you

Picking a major may seem like one of the most important decisions of your life, but in all honesty, it isn't. Law schools and corporate jobs are willing to take students from any major, so **unless you are trying to go to Med School, feel free to study what interests you**. Having a strong GPA is more important than fitting in with the "ideal" major, so having a 3.7 in Gov will actually benefit you more than having a 3.3 in Econ.

Dartmouth has over 50 majors to choose from, and they are all structured fairly similarly. Most majors include prerequisites, **1-2 introductory courses, 6-8 intermediate courses, and a culminating experience** (your Senior Seminar). Senior Seminars often consist of a term-long research paper, but by senior year, students are hopefully well-versed enough in their fields that the paper is not an issue. You are required to declare a major by your sophomore spring, which should give you enough time to shop around to find your best fit. A helpful stat: the 5 most popular majors at Dartmouth are Economics, Government, Biology, English, and History.

Declaring a Major:

To declare you must obtain three major cards from the Registrar, map out the classes you are planning to take, and have it signed by an advisor. One card goes back to the Registrar, one card goes to your major department, and you keep the third (so you actually only need two cards). **Usually, people have no idea the exact classes they are planning to take for the next two years,** so the classes you choose sophomore year are there just to prove that you actually have some sort of plan to finish the major. Unfortunately, this causes serious frenzy senior spring when seniors remember that they have to re-file their major cards with the correct classes they took.

If you are planning on double majoring, realize you have to file 6 cards, and fill out one extra page of paperwork. Finally, for those who couldn't handle the double major requirements, you can always choose to add a minor, which consists of about half the classes; but it's like baseball, no one respects the minors.

Thesis:

Dartmouth does offer some modifications to this process, however. The first is receiving honors in your major. Students can elect to **write a thesis** their senior year in lieu of their culminating experience. Students should apply junior year, and then spend the next twelve months of their life not having fun and writing an absurdly long paper. Examples include "The Dollar as a Reserve Currency in the Interwar Years" (History department), a novel about a summer camp in Maine (English department), and "Opposition and Revolution in Egypt" (Government department). While your respective department will often pay for you to fly around the world to research your topic, **the all-nighters that people pull to ensure they meet deadlines never seems worth it**.

Modified Major:

Another variation offered at Dartmouth is the **Modified Major**. Some majors will allow you to modify your major with classes from another department. This is for the students who weren't smart enough to double major and realized that minors sucked, so they decided to create a Frankenstein-bastard-child of a major. People will claim that their "Engineering modified with Creative Writing" Major is legit, but it just sounds like you withdrew from your mid-level electromagnetism class. As long as you can make some sort of logical argument as to why your classes fit together, modifying your major with something easy (like studio art) is a possibility.

Senior Fellowship:

Finally, Dartmouth also has the **Senior Fellowship**. Each year, a very small number of seniors are selected to become Senior Fellows. The program, instituted by President Hopkins, is intended for students whose academic interest goes beyond the scope of the Dartmouth curriculum. Fellows take their senior year off from taking classes, are not required to take a major, and spend their senior year researching a topic of their choice. One Senior Fellow, for example, wrote a book about the evolution (devolution?) of the music industry over the past fifty years, and was able to fly back and forth between Nashville and New York, interviewing some big names in the music industry.

Top 10 Professors

Based on devotion to undergraduate learning and impressiveness of résumé

1	Donald Pease	English 047
2	Robert Fesen	Astronomy 002/003
3	Dean Lacy	Government 030
4	Meir Kohn	Economics 026
5	Bruce Sacerdote	Economics 046
6	Larry Crocker	Philosophy 050
7	Dale Turner	Native American Studies 045
8	Ford Evans	Theater 026
9	Jody Diamond	Asian & Middle Eastern Studies 018
10	William Wohlforth	Government 056

Top 10 Distribs

(based on balance of difficulty and intellectual stimulation)

1	Movement Fundamentals
2	American Drama / Fiction
3	Sociology 010
4	Astronomy 001/002/003
5	Physics 002
6	Indonesian Gamelan
7	Russian 013
8	Native American Studies
9	Math 005
10	Economics 026

Corporate Recruiting
A Masochist's Guide

You are receiving these words from a person who did it. Let's start from the top: the process is grueling, competitive, and most importantly, incredibly awful to talk about with other people. **The first rule of corporate recruiting is that you do not talk about corporate recruiting.** Your friends who are interviewing with you will become more competitive; your friends who are not will think you are a chotch. But this op-ed is between me, a guy who did it, and you, a person who wants to. So listen closely, make a deal with the devil, and hope for the best.

When you came to college, you were so bright-eyed. You wanted to change the world: you were going to be pre-med, get a 4.0, cure cancer, start a company, and write a book! 1% of you will keep this fire alive and leave college making an actual difference in the world, and I commend you; the rest of you will be bankers or consultants. Let me rephrase that, **the rest of you will want to be bankers or consultants; some of you will have to settle for law school**. Don't get me wrong, I thought I was going to go to law school too when I came to college – it's an admirable profession, and your mother will be extremely proud. Then one day, I realized I could "Skip Go" and just do banking. I didn't even know the country I am currently vacationing in existed six months ago... let's go!

Now that I have convinced you, let's talk about the specifics at Dartmouth. **Career Services is actually very good at what they do, and they will help you find something**. Go to them to look for job opportunities, network with alumni, edit cover letters, shorten resumes, etc. The first round of recruiting occurs over Sophomore Summer (enjoy your freshman summer, but remember that "lawn-mower specialist" might not help your employment plans). Companies will hold interviews on campus for internships offered primarily during your junior winter. By the end of June, you will need to submit a cover letter (a one page introduction that explains why you want to work at said company and what skills you can bring with you) and a résumé (if you don't know what this is, it is already too late for you). The second round of recruiting occurs during **junior winter** for the following summer, and the final round of recruiting occurs during **senior fall** for full-time positions after graduating. The process is almost always the same: cover letter, résumé, interview, repeat. There will be a day where most of the applications are due, so make sure to keep that in mind, and don't start the night before – making sure everything uploads correctly is stressful enough.

So you know when to turn everything in, I'll give you a few tips that helped me land my job. Let's start with your résumé. Sorry to say, but **GPA does matter for landing that interview**. The easiest thing to do is just to crush school, but if that isn't an option, change your major. Dartmouth is a liberal arts school so we don't have a finance major, and recruiters know that. You can be any major and land a job in finance or consulting; it just takes a good résumé and great interview skills. A couple things to remember: limit your résumé to one page in length, and do not include a photo of yourself, no matter how good looking you think you are. Employers look at résumés for maybe thirty seconds, so make sure everything you put on there is important and to the point.

If you are lucky enough to land an interview, you might want to practice what you are going to say before you walk through the door. I recommend the *Vault Guide to Finance Interviews* for bankers and *Case in Point: Complete Case Interview Preparation* for consultants. You should write out the answers to as many questions as possible and practice going through your responses, but don't get into "study groups" with your friends to work on it. Remember if you talk about it with your friends, you will look like a chotch. The interview process is long, and if you do well there will likely be three or more rounds you may have to go through including the famed "Super Day," so be prepared from the beginning.

Once you have crushed the interview, enjoy the benefits. Your hair will start to look better/greasier, your clothes will immediately become nicer, and you will never ever sleep! Embrace becoming part of the machine, and realize that the sooner you accept it as inevitable, the more time you have to prepare your résumé.

The second rule of corporate recruiting: Wharton Sucks.

The D-Plan

Go Abroad, Young People!

The D-Plan is not for everyone... at least at first. Most people initially bemoan the prospect of leaving the safe Dartmouth bubble even for one of their terms (let alone two). There are consistently two specific concerns that accompany these worries:

First: I'm going to miss my friends so much when I'm gone. And then when I come back, I'll miss them so much when they're gone! *Wahhh!*

Second: How am I ever going to have a steady relationship at this school when my significant other and I are always off at different times?! *Wahhh!*

Fear not, you insatiable whiners! Your fears can be addressed quite easily.

1. Let's see how you feel after spending three straight terms on campus with these "great" friends of yours. The reality is that like most things untreated by Botox, friends get old and dull after extended periods of time. These terms abroad will be a welcome respite from the maniacal clutches of your college friends. Not to mention, when you come back from abroad, these friends will seem shiny and new!

2. Monogamy is so 1994. Are you really going to cry over your freshman love when you're in the strong and supple arms of an Italian man on your transfer term in Florence? Will you really remember that cute girl next door when you're subway-rubbing with a British girl on the Tube? *Answer: No.*

The D-Plan simply provides **too many great opportunities to not like it**. Dartmouth will be there when you get back from your terms abroad and if anything, will seem even more fantastic. Don't miss out on the opportunity of taking a FSP (Foreign Study Program) in Barcelona an LSA (Language Study Abroad) in Paris, a transfer term in New Zealand, or an off-term in New York City, just because you think you'll miss Dartmouth. Fortune favors the bold, and nowhere is this more true than with the opportunity for exploration that the D-Plan provides.

10 Things You Must Do

1. Buy a Killington Season Pass ($300)

2. Close down 1902 Room

3. Open Lou's at 6 a.m.

4. Heckle at a Men's Soccer game

5. Fort Lou's at 4 a.m., heckle the night shift

6. Pond hockey on Occom in the winter

7. Learn to play squash (not the veggie)

8. Rush a secret society

9. Complete the Ledyard Challenge

10. Get an Un'dun whippits punch card

Barcelona Transfer Term
Academy of Liberal and Beaux-Arts

What can I say about ALBA that hasn't already been said about a neuroscience class at Dartmouth? It's full of athletes and led by people that seem like they don't care. Classes meet once a week for two hours with a strict attendance requirement of seven out of ten classes. Many of these classes have up to as many as three field trips that replace in-class sessions. This gem of a three credit term (a full Dartmouth term) is run through Portland State University, which obviously holds its students to an extremely high standard. If you play your cards right, you can have 6-day weekends by scheduling all your classes on one day ("tough guy Tuesday").

Terms Available: *All*

Difficulty: *A+*

Campus: *F*
The "campus" is actually an apartment that is rented by the people who run the program. Although the classroom and makeshift library offer hilariously inadequate academic facilities, you won't be spending much time here, so it's not a big deal.

Accommodation: *B+*
Everyone gets their own apartment in the city of Barcelona, many of them adjacent to a nude beach.

Dining: *NR* (100% restaurant dining)

Popular Excursions:
The **beach near the Olympic village** is an incredible place to spend a day, and the Mediterranean is great for swimming. There are two club promoters who have the job of getting deals at a new club every night for all Americans studying abroad - one named Kike ("key-kay") and the other named Kyke ("key-kay"). Don't worry, if you have even thought about studying abroad in Barcelona, they will find you on Facebook – they are vultures. Be sure to **hit up Las Ramblas and catch an F.C. Barcelona game at the Camp Nou.**

Beijing FSP

Beijing Normal University

While Beijing offers the most interesting cultural and social experience, this program brings more academic stress than the typical term at Dartmouth. The native speakers would laugh at that statement, as they flawlessly breezed through classes. The rest of us found ourselves up at 5 a.m. at the campus McDonald's eating a #7 while dripping grease over thousands of flashcards. For those of you who can accept the "failure" of a B+, the nightlife and sightseeing opportunities will keep you happily busy for the entire ten-week term. For AMES and AMELL majors/minors out there, upon returning from this program you will have three credits under your belt.

Terms available: *Summer and Fall*

Difficulty: *B*

Campus: *B-*

Accommodation: *A*
The dorms are converted hotel rooms complete with maid service, air conditioning, full bathrooms, local television, and two full sized beds.

Dining: *NR* (all restaurant dining)
The local Chinese restaurants specialize in various traditional Chinese cuisine. However, once you venture out of walking distance into other neighborhoods, you can find international cuisine varying in quality and price. Go to **"Pyro Pizza"** in Wudaokou, **"The Saddle"** in Sanlitun, and **"Serve the People"** in Sanlitun.

Popular excursions:

The FSP director will organize trips for 8 out of the 10 weekends, and students get to see every major sightseeing masterpiece (Great Wall, Summer Palace, Inner Mongolia, etc.). Students have ample free time to roam around Beijing. At night, students have their pick of going to Beijing's hottest and sweatiest dance clubs (**Vicks, Mix, Club Banana, and Propaganda**), or sipping drinks at one of the sports, karaoke, or wine bars in Sanlitun (**Shooters, La Bamba, or Scarlett**).

London Study Abroad

Royal Holloway

Ever wonder what it would have actually been like to go to school at Hogwarts? If so, then the Royal Holloway study abroad program is as close as you're ever going to get! The main building is a castle, the classes are taught by professors with foreign accents, and the campus is heavily fortified. Just replace the butter beer with snake-bites (the drink), the wands with No. 7 pencils, and the enchanted forest with a highway, and you're basically there. The best thing is, instead of class every day of the week (what calendar was the wizarding world on anyway?), it only meets twice! This gives you plenty of time to explore Egham (don't) and London.

Terms Available: *Winter*

Difficulty: *A+*

Campus: *B+*
Located in Egham, Surrey, RHUL is a twenty-five-minute cab ride (forty minutes by train) outside of London proper. The campus, located on a gigantic hill, is actually beautiful. It contains scenic views and pretty amazing architecture (yes, there actually is a castle).

Accommodations: *A*
The dorms are all singles with double beds, a full bathroom, and a full kitchen in the hall.

Dining: *B* (Mediocre, overpriced cafeteria style food)

Popular Excursions

The first club in London anyone needs to hit is tropical-themed Mahiki. I've blown more money and lost more clothing at this place than Tiger Woods in a strip poker game, and I'm sure the celebrities that frequent Mahiki can say the same. When you're not out drinking during the nighttime, you should be out drinking during the daytime. Church, a club only open from 12 p.m.-4 p.m. on Sundays (the hours normal people go to church), has cheap drinks, a huge dance floor, and a comedian performing throughout.

New Zealand Transfer Term
University of Otago

New Zealand is a spectacular country full of incredible history, people, flora, fauna, and partying. The southern most part of the south Island is called Dunedin, and is a small city that is home to a huge university called the University of Otago. The transfer term to this part of the world is ideal since it is in the winter at Dartmouth but is the summer for the southern hemisphere. Since the University of Otago is in its summer session, Dunidan is less crowded than usual but still very much a party city.

Terms Available: *Winter*

Difficulty: *A+*
While one has the choice of taking classes that range from New Zealand history to post-modern philosophy, the courses aren't particularly rigorous.

Campus: *A-*

Accommodations: *A-*

Dining: *D*

Popular Excursions

The nightlife of Dunidan is as fantastic as a Cher concert! Because it's a college town, the entire place is chock full of student bars, karaoke lounges, small restaurants, and dorm parties. You and around fifteen other Dartmouth students can eat, drink, and club to your heart's content. On weekends, you and a group can head to bigger cities like **Christchurch and Queenstown** for fantastic clubs and restaurants.

Here are must do's: Bungee jumping and skydiving in Queenstown, wine tasting in Nelson, seeing the Flora around Christchurch, and taking the **Lord of the Rings Tour** around Queenstown.

*New Zealanders are probably the greatest thing about New Zealand. Nowhere in the world will you find nicer, more accepting, or funnier locals. As an additional bonus, their accents are simply adorable.

V

Freshmen
Dormitories

"Home is the place where, when you have to go there, they have to take you in."

Robert Frost, 1915

The Choates

"The Penitentiary"

Pretty much the only "penitence" the residents of this infamously ragey dorm cluster give is directed toward their one-room-double roommates, whom they booted on the night before. Otherwise the only thing they are actually sorry for is well, partying. The rooms in this cinder-block cluster are small, dingy, cramped and feature the privacy of a jail-house community shower. Although still convicted as one of the worst dorms to physically "live" in, it is actually one of the best dorms to live "in". It could be the proximity to frat row or the "what else could we possibly mess up" attitude, but although its residents move on every year, the notorious stigma lives on in those creaky pipes and moldy walls.

You can't ignore the fact that the Choates are fun. If you are lucky enough to be placed there, embrace it. Parents may not like to hear this but come on... welcome to college.

Alternatively, these dorms are by far the most uncomfortable to live in on campus. For those of you who haven't caught on to the general motif of this description, the rooms are small and reminiscent of a correctional facility, albeit a fun one.

Building   D
Amenities   D
Location   B+
Greek Factor   A
Social Presence A+
Overall   *B*

Keywords:
Frat Row, Novack

East Wheelock

"The Purgatory"

You must be really excited to be at Dartmouth, no but really excited. You crushed all your extracurricular activities in high school: you were the president of the student body, took five (5) AP classes, and were president of six (6) other student organizations! You saw that application for East Wheelock, and you thought to yourself, "Of course I would love to meet with professors in small intimate settings every four-to-six weeks! I'm an intellectual!" What a mistake: realize the group of people you are self-segregating yourself into when you do this.

The rooms in East Wheelock, however, are huge, and the facilities are nice. If you want to have a fun floor that goes out on Fridays and Saturdays, put down the application right now, but if that isn't your scene East Wheelock might be a great fit. There is a great snack bar in there.

Building   A+
Amenities   A+
Location   B-
Geek Factor   A+
Social Presence   D
Overall   B+

Keywords:
Far, Gym, Sober

FRESHMEN DORMS

Fahey-McLane

"Fahey-McLame"

Built in 2006, this small cluster immediately garnered the reputation as the best overall freshman dorm. It unfortunately lost some of that luster within less than a decade of existence: the spacious and cozy two room doubles, which made Fahey-McLane such a great dorm, have transformed into cramped, two-room triples. This now doubles the chance that the roommate you share a bedroom with will be a snorer, have a frequently visiting girlfriend, or be a total idiot.

A fan of Fahey-McLane would point out its phenomenal location. Its proximity to Frat Row, the Library, and FoCo is unmatched. Finally, the bathrooms and showers never get cold and are clean enough to shower barefoot!

Sleeping soberly in Fahey-McLane is oddly difficult, but not for the same reasons that plague the Choates. The bedroom doors close automatically and slam every single time they shut, so it feels more like sleeping through a scene from *Shoot 'em Up* rather than a small town nestled in the woods of New Hampshire. Also, some claim the residents are lame due to their haughtily isolationist attitudes and lack of floor solidarity (although this obviously changes with time).

Building   A
Amenities   B-
Location   A
Greek Factor   B+
Social Presence B+
Overall   B+

Keywords:
Triples, New, Sexy

McLaughlin

"Hotel Dartmouth"

Barring the location, the McLaughlin cluster is arguably the best dorm to live in on campus. It is more comfortable to live in than its namesake/benefactor's Sleep Comfort™ beds are to sleep in (look it up). Funny enough, the U.S Green Energy Council honored McLaughlin's buildings in 2008 for their overall sustainable nature, even though it was widely reported that more polar bears drowned there in 2009 than in the Arctic and every zoo in America combined. The cluster also boasts a "mini-Green," where socially awkward freshmen and kids enjoying self-toss Frisbee can be spotted on warm spring days.

A fan of the dorm would mention its easily accessible elevators, its Anything-But-Clothes parties, and its hook-up-friendly rooms. The close proximity to Dick's House keeps the residents' supply of penicillin fully stocked, so they are generally the least likely to get you sick on campus.

Haters would complain that because it is so easy to hook up in the two-room-double rooms that their friends who occupy this dorm are prone to settling down in the dating scene quite early. Also, the residents' sustainable high-horse they tend to ride can induce an impatient peer to throw a can of beer in the offender's face, and then litter.

Building   A
Amenities   A
Location   C
Greek Factor   C+
Social Presence A
Overall   *A-*

Keywords:
Far, Fresh, Fun

The River

"The Cliff"

Located behind the Tuck Business and Thayer Engineering schools, these architectural masterpieces were built in 1962, a construction date that appropriately reflects their dilapidated appearance. The River cluster, is for all intents and purposes, a black hole; it's inconveniently far away, upon getting there you're probably not going to leave, and it was discovered by Stephen Hawking. If you find yourself living in the River your freshman year, don't worry too much - there's always next year.

A fan of the River might cite that its proximity to the Tuck Dining Hall provides a tasty option - just be prepared to pay DA$H. The three-room doubles also allow for excessive Beirut before heading to Frat Row and getting smoked in pong. "It is, Sir, as I have said, a shitty dorm. And yet there are those who love it."

A hater of the River would point to its awful location while simultaneously ordering Boloco for the fourth night in a row. The walk to on-campus dining is just too damn far.

Building   B-

Amenities   B

Location   D

Greek Factor   C-

Social Presence D

Overall   *C*

Keywords:
Far, FML, Delivery

Russell Sage/Butterfield

"Sussell Rage"

Constructed in 1922, the Russell Sage cluster is classic Dartmouth on the outside and classic 1970's on the inside. By this we mean that the outside is old and stoic, while the inside blasts outdated music and everyone gets around on roller-skates. And by that we mean the outside is in no way representative of the inside. For some reason, this dorm carries the reputation as the "ragiest" dorm on campus, illustrated by its nickname: "Sussell Rage" (see what they did there?). The most fun-loving freshmen pine to be placed in Russell Sage because of its party-like reputation, while library-frequenting freshmen pine to be placed in Russell Sage because of its proximity to Baker.

The rooms are unflattering, but classic college. Two-room corner-triples are cramped and lack privacy, while the scent of mold is hard to ignore. No one seems to care, though. The location is prime and the company is typically friendly. While the late-night noise may bother some people, you really can't do anything about it; so, embrace it! The solidarity created in and between floors within the Cluster is rivaled only by the Choates.

Building   B
Amenities   A-
Location   A+
Greek Factor B+
Social Presence A
Overall   *A-*

Keywords:
Frat, Libs, FoCo

FRESHMEN DORMS

The Archetypes
Who You May (not) Meet in Your Dorm...

The "Social Butterfly"

For some, freshman year marks a new beginning. Never drank before? Weren't that nice of a person in high school? Whatever. College provides opportunities to reinvent the wheel, if you are the wheel. In every dorm, it will be easy to follow the sound of music and/or scent of "tobacco" to the room of these overexcited hosts. Thoughts of "College" and "No parents!" abound, these kids will be the life of the freshman pre-game, candidly snapping pictures, while simultaneously holding a funnel and executing a mobile Facebook album upload. While often irritating, somewhat toolish, and likely to experience the ol' Parkhurst, freshman year needs these underage Sociology of Keystone majors to keep doing what they're doing. So, here's to you, Social Butterfly—by the end of freshman year, you budding socialites will be the big shots lamenting, "I remember my first beer..."

Aloof West-Coaster

Intent on drawing the best and brightest from across the globe, Dartmouth attracts a solid student contingency from the Autonomous Region of California. One can easily identify these wannabe secessionists sporting "NorCal" or "SoCal" t-shirts and complaining about the 'shitty' Hanover weather. No one cares that In-N-Out is better than Wendy's and no one cares that you can surf the Pacific in the morning, ski Tahoe in the afternoon, and nurse your glaucoma in the evening (although that is pretty sweet). Like most students, these Aloof West-Coasters will eventually adapt. Unlike most students, they will occasionally consider transferring to USC.

Overeager Beaver

In High School, the Overeager Beaver was very impressive. They were the president of every organization, they did community service, and they definitely got a 4.0. But what they don't understand is that everyone at Dartmouth was that kid at their respective high schools. Here is our disclaimer: do not try to be the same person you were in high school when you come to Dartmouth; college is a time to change and grow-up, so embrace it.

I can't figure out how the Overeager Beaver has enough time to be a part of so many organizations. The only explanation is that they use a device similar to Emma Watson's time-turner that she used to not get made fun of at Brown. They will be a part of everything. Student assembly - obviously. Tucker Foundation - naturally. The Aires/Dodecs - unquestionably. Good luck not burning out. Seriously, imagine what conversations with these kids are like:

You: *"Hey, are you going out tonight?"*
Beaver: *"Tonight, on a Wednesday? Of course not! I have like 400 pages of reading for Gov 3! I'll be in the study room down the hall though if you want to do work together or something!"*

By all means, join students groups at Dartmouth, but realize that you aren't Superman. The Overeager Beaver will spend his or her next four years at Dartmouth running from meeting to meeting inevitably looking over some of the best parts of the experience.

New York All Girls School Girl

You will know her when you see her. She may look like the girl in middle school who didn't care that you existed. She'll have an oversized bag made by some guy whose name you can't pronounce. She will have a fur-lined coat for the winter, Hunter rain boots for the spring, and "cute" plaid shirts for the fall. Her sunglasses will be too large for her face, and she will obviously own a Mac, never a Dell. One thing you can be sure of is that she will definitely have something to complain to you about.

Her: *"Oh my gawd! I tried to go shopping at Juliana's, and they didn't have anything worth buying! I am sick and tired of shopping online! Sometimes I wish we were back in the City!"*
You: *"Cool."*

But don't stereotype her; she's been through a lot. Her investment-banking father recently sold their house in the Hamptons to buy a farmhouse in Vermont (damn the recession). Within a week, she will have found all of the girls in the grade that are exactly like her, and they will become the Queens of Facetime as if it were a Lindsay Lohan movie. That means eating salads at Collis, ellipticals at the gym, and going on pong dates with brothers. By sophomore fall she will burst into your room in tears, Dirt Cowboy cup in hand, grieving over not getting into her sorority of choice (Kappa). Some people just have all the luck.

The High School Hero

From day one, they'll be decked out in their high school football shirt and lacrosse sweatpants eager to show you that they still "got it". About half these guys will join the rugby team; the other half will make a big show of going to the gym, totally crushing club lax or soccer, and looking for opportunities to display their athletic prowess. They can run faster, jump higher, and beat you in any sport... (at the club level... maybe). They're generally fine to hang out with until you somehow provoke them into declaring about how much more athletic they are than you. If you want to have some fun, call them a NARP and see what happens. Not surprisingly, many fraternities have their fair share of these people. Over time, many of these would-be superstars channel their competitive energy into more fratty pursuits such as pong, whiffle ball, quick-sixes, and Fifa. This guy does have one huge upshot though: **your intramural sports team will love to have him around.**

You: *"Hey, I didn't know you played [X sport]. Are you on the team?*
Hero: *"No, I totally would have been, but my knee just wouldn't hold up."*
You: *"Oh, so are you playing club?"*
Hero: *"Yeah, for now. Most of those kids are garbage though. My team won States last year, so it's a bit of a joke. The coach told me to keep rehabbing and maybe I can walk on next year."*

New England Prepster

The prep school graduate will arrive fully ready for college in New England with his J. Crew pea coat, Nantucket Red shorts, Sperry's, Oversand Vehicle Permit t-shirt from the Vineyard as well as the obligatory Deerfield lax penny, Belmont Hill hat, or Choate pullover, which he'll still wear well after freshman year.

One special talent these guys have (especially the boarding school crowd) is the ability to transform an average dorm room into a palace. While you were riding your bike to Dwight D. Eisenhower Memorial High School, he was busy perfecting the art of dorm life at Exeter. If you show even the slightest curiosity, you'll be regaled with stories about the time he and his bros chanted, "Safety school," at the Avon Old Farms game or the time he packed the fattest lip you've ever seen during Prize Day. Sick, dude.

UGA: Friend or Foe?

A UGA aficionado weighs in

Now let me first establish that I'm more puff-puff-pass than Jigglypuff so don't think I'm some unreliable, suck-up source. I have stolen bikes from FoCo because the walk home is too damn long. I have farted in the Tower Room because Sunja's a bitch on the bowels. I live my life in the UV without sunblock, and I'm proud of it.

And I'm also proud of this opinion: **UGA's are your friends, your homies, your resources**, however you want to call it. Now I'm only evaluating freshmen UGA's because upper-classmen UGA's are a joke. They have the easiest f*ckin' job on campus, save that random-ass info desk when you walk into The Hop.

Pardon that digression. Yeah, freshmen UGA's are your friends. They provide a much needed structure in your early weeks at school and despite the weekly meetings' eventual chafe, Floor Meetings give you great opportunity to (a) chirp at the hotties on your floor, (b) snag some free food and (c) develop your first network of people that's oh-so-helpful when you're looking for a layup. You'll soon learn that chirping at hotties over blitz or even in passing is much, much creepier. And free food is very available on campus but for the most part, it's awkward to obtain because you're crashing either a charitable or annoying organization.

Also I know there are horror stories out there of UGA's busting up your SICK room party or Good Samming (see appendix) you when you were "definitely sober". But this really doesn't happen that often and if it does, you probably deserve it. Why get so f*ckin' rowdy in your room when we have frats for that? And if you're wandering around the floor letting General Tso fight all over the ground, then you're grim and need to be less sloppy. Let Diversions be a lesson and you'll meet some new buddies there, plus have the sweet pick-up line that "you got Good Sammed". See, everyone wins?

Don't hate on your freshmen UGA. He or she is there for you and helps you in ways you won't ever acknowledge unless you write a piece like this.

Thanks, Freshmen UGA's - you're the best.

Facebook Perspectives
From the Class of '15 Facebook Group*

'15 Girl #1 - *Subject: random*
okkayy this has absolutely nothing to do with dartmouth but I'm wonderngg if any of you guys can help mee. Does anyonee in here go to the hamptons in long island for afterprom and can possibly help me find a house!
'15 #2: *theyre like all gone now lol*
'15 Girl #1: *Ahhh ugh I know I've been searching for days!*
'15 #2: *i gave up but it worked out anyway for me lol*
'15 Girl #1: *Wait u got a house?*
'15 #2: *my friend did but its in smithtown. idk how but she did lol*
'15 Girl #1: *Waaait! Give me details! How many bedroom/ does it have a pool or hottub?*

-First World Problems...

*****

'15 Girl #1- *Subject: hi!*
hey everyone! Is there some site/list/something that breaks down the "personality" of each frat? (ie how do you know which one to join besides just reputation?)
'15 Guy #1: *This is something only a current junior/senior would really know about.*

-Wise beyond your years...

*****

'15 Guy #1 - *Subject: I chose Dartmouth over_____*
For me it was duke, northwestern, and uchicago
'15 Girl #1: *I applied to Dartmouth Early Decision. Why not make the right choice early on?*
'15 Guy #2: *Brown, UChicago, and Williams.*
My dream was to bleed green all my life, so it was basically a no-brainer when I heard I got in off the waitlist :)

-Hanover > Chi Town. Also, wise beyond your years...

*we may embellish a lot of things, but these quotes are from actual '15s

FRESHMEN DORMS

VI

Dartmouth
Social Life

"This is what a college should look like."

Dwight D. Eisenhower, 1953

Hanover Police

"H-Po"

In the words of a former IFC president, "If Safety and Security is the benevolent parental figure who keeps us from succumbing to our own worst instincts, H-Po is the crazy uncle who comes over every so often and causes absolute mayhem on the whole household."

Every few years, **H-Po decides that Dartmouth's overly-regulated, completely self-contained social scene is a threat to public order and an affront to decent society** (or they just get really bored). With an enthusiasm normally reserved for meth-heads and murderers, Hanover's finest descend onto campus and issue arrest warrants and indictments against the evil-doers who dare to drink underage and the criminal organizations that shelter them. And don't think that they don't have the training or manpower to do it. Hanover is one of the most over-policed towns in New Hampshire and boasts several SWAT-certified officers. Stories of **H-Po's exploits on campus are almost as comical as they are disheartening**. Frequently cited examples include the police chief and his top lieutenant hiding in the woods trying to detect hazing (some students were practicing a speech), and one officer using night vision goggles to track down drunk kids on the golf course. Fortunately, the college doesn't want H-Po on campus, and a lot of town officials don't either. H-Po also probably gets tired of hunting drunk nineteen-year-olds and the subsequent mountain of paperwork. Therefore, these periods tend to operate in cycles.

Things to know:

Diversions Program:

The Diversions Program is given to first-time underage violators of alcohol laws. For $400 (roughly ¼ of that if you're arrested outside of Hanover), you get to go to a day-long class on alcohol abuse instead of getting charged with possession of alcohol. **Diversions does NOT go on your record.**

Minor in Possession of Alcohol charge:

If you get arrested again for alcohol violations, you are ineligible for Diversions. Don't panic, a minor in possession of alcohol charge in New Hampshire is the **equivalent of a speeding ticket**. It is a Civil Violation. Your life will not come to an end. Relax.

Talking to Police:

Always remember your rights. **You have the right to say nothing about what you did or did not do**. So many Dartmouth students either panic at the first sight of a badge and spill the beans or try to talk themselves out of trouble and end up getting arrested. Greek houses also don't appreciate it when someone claims they were drinking at a specific house and then that house gets charged for providing alcohol to minors.

Names to know:

Nick Giaccone, Police Chief:

The Hammer of Justice. Giaccone has been the chief for over fifteen years and served on the force for a long time prior to that. In winter of 2010, he tried to implement sting operations in the fraternities. That backfired enormously, so he launched a crackdown that resulted in multiple charges against individuals and organizations. The College administration and student leaders worked with the police and the town government to return to a more normal level of enforcement.

Detective Captain Frank Moran:

Robin to Giaccone's Batman. If you're ever an officer in a Greek house and your house gets investigated, you get to talk to this guy.

Officer Jeff Ballard:

What the Ghostbusters were for ghosts, Jeff Ballard is for underage drinking. Well known for his "enthusiasm and dedication" for police work, you'll just have to experience him for yourselves (which shouldn't be too difficult). The next time you see him, ask to check out his nightstick and riot gloves. Actually, don't. That won't end well at all.

*NWA said it best...

SOCIAL LIFE

Office of Judicial Affairs

Beware.

The worst possible name you can see in a the "sender" column of an email is "The Office of Judicial Affairs". The Office of Judicial Affairs is responsible for dealing with students or organizations that are accused of doing something wrong. Whether an individual is caught cheating on a test or a fraternity is accused of serving alcohol to minors, all roads lead to the Office of Judicial Affairs (OJA).

The OJA is easily the most poorly run branch at Dartmouth. It's way too bureaucratic, it's understaffed and slow, and the people there are basically Autobots. The **OJA staff treats the "Dartmouth Student Handbook" like it's Hammurabi's Code** - when a rule is broken, there needs to be a punishment, no questions asked. It's safe to say that if you were playing a Dartmouth version of "Apples to Apples," and the category word was "Hell," playing the "Office of Judicial Affairs" card would get you the win every time.

If you ever find yourself in trouble, however, here's how the process will work. You'll be contacted by OJA saying they are "investigating" an incident and want a statement from you, so they can decide if "the matter needs to be pursued further". What this actually means is, "We're going to charge you with what you've been accused of, and we've already decided that we are going to pursue the matter." In terms of these written statements, the best advice is to just deny, deny, deny. **Any admission of guilt, and you're toast.**

Next, you'll be called into the office for a hearing. Prior to the start of the hearing, everyone will be incredibly friendly and try to make you feel comfortable. They will offer you a soda, they will ask you questions about your classes, and they will even offer you candy. **DO NOT fall for these tactics**. They want you buttered up and feeling comfy, so you say something stupid at your hearing. Remember how nice the witch was at first in Hansel and Gretel? As soon as they trusted her she literally tried to eat them. Whatever you do, don't let your guard down at this place.

The most frustrating aspect of the whole process are the boards that oversee your case. If it's a minor infraction, you are placed in front of a group of five "unbiased" students who decide your fate. Ever seen Animal House? Remember the kid who runs the student court in that movie? Those are the types of kids that sit on these boards at Dartmouth. They aren't exactly looking to bail you out.

*welp, see ya later

Unfortunately, you're actually lucky if you get the student board. The other option is a board with faculty on it. The school claims this is a board of your "peers". This makes perfect sense, 'cause you know, **a sixty year-old Economics teacher from Russia really knows what life is like for a college student**. The fact is, you're pretty much screwed before you go into these hearings. The teachers don't feel satisfied unless you are punished. After hours of incredibly dumb questions from the faculty, you inevitably end up getting in trouble. You feel like a witch in a Salem Witch Trial.

As terrible as I've made the Office sound, the truth is, **as long as you aren't caught cheating, the punishments aren't too bad**. While the OJA is incredibly harsh on organizations such as fraternities, it is far more lenient on individual students. The advice I've given, however, is all true. Your best strategy is to deny, these people are not your friends, and they will go by the book and punish you if you admit anything.

The Dartmouth X

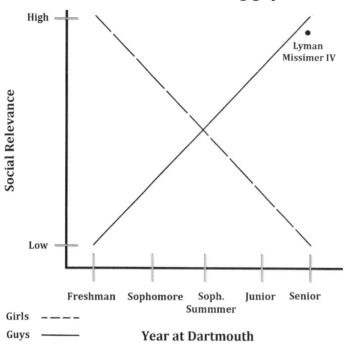

The Letter X: succinct, elusive, sensual. While the letter X may just be the twenty-fourth letter of the Latin alphabet to you, it means something entirely different for Dartmouth students. Now, I'm not saying that the X doesn't occur at other colleges because it in fact does; it's just that other colleges weren't clever enough to give it a name.

The Dartmouth X, at its most basic level, is a graph of social relevancy based on simple supply and demand. Freshmen boys enter at the bottom left corner of the graph. They have to ask how to get beers, and they can't even keep a pong ball on table. HOW EMBARASSING! But have no fear, as time goes on, boys slowly move to the top corner of the graph. You will become wittier, your hair will fall in place more naturally, and your muscles will grow.* As for girls, pretend its opposite day and reread the above statement (and follow the twitter @existentialseniorgirlproblems). The beauty of this interaction is the famed Sophomore Summer. Playing fields even out, and everyone meets in the middle, pun intended.

*citation needed

Top Ten Dartmouth Alumni

Ever heard of them?

1. Robert Frost
2. Theodore Seuss Geisel
3. Stephen Colbert
4. Tim Geithner
5. Steve Mandel
6. Jeff Immelt
7. Chris Miller
8. Meryl Streep
9. Henry Paulson
10. Leon Black

The "Pong Date"

The Do's and Don'ts

Despite your best intentions, you will have many pong dates during college. You'll feel like a tool, and you will be. But that's OK, because everybody else in the basement who's judging you has done the exact same thing before. This discussion will be in four parts. The first details how to get to a pong date. The second and third are do's and don'ts, and the fourth details how to parlay from a pong date to a horizontal date.

How to get to a pong date:

This can happen any number of ways. The best way is for it to happen organically. You need a fourth, and s/he's standing there. That's a good enough reason. Or you just took your final for Gov number whatever. You've gotta play after that. **Don't blitz them and ask if they want to play pong sometimes.** You don't want to have such an embarrassing request in writing. Keep it verbal, and keep it casual. Everything about pong has to stay casual.

Do:

There are many things to do during a pong date. First of all, it has to be a series. There are many reasons for this. Everybody's awkward enough that one game's worth of social lubricant just isn't going to do it. And the girl's going to feel like a "real classy lady," and the guy's going to feel like a skeaze if either of them makes the effort to hook up with the other person after just one game of pong. Everybody else in the basement will complain about how you're hogging table space. They're just jealous because you're getting action tonight, and they're not. Also: **have a totally cute celebration.** This one you might actually want to think of in your spare time. You need to do something cool when you hit/sink. Ideally, you'll do something for a sink, and something different for a hit. **Bumping butts is always a winner.** Explosions on a pound are OK, but will work in times of desperation. Air-fiving from a very close distance will win you some points.

Don't:

Don't make out during the game. Even if the other person really wants to. Just don't. This isn't exhibitionism. It's pong. And you're subjecting the other team to a cruel and unusual punishment, especially if they're also on a date. You're leaving them with three options: 1) make out as well, but they're probably not going to 2) watch you make out, which isn't that fun 3) talk about something, but really, what are they going to talk about? So don't make out during the game. **Don't get overly competitive**, either. Knock over some cups and laugh it off. Sink on a serve? Great. How funny! If you're stone-faced, then you might end up hugging your pillow. Don't criticize the other person when they f*ck up. Compliment sandwich it if you have to criticize.

Parlay:

This requires subtlety and tact. If you're vibing really well (and you can tell if you're vibing and you can tell if you're not), you need to invent an excuse to get him/her to a more suitable location. Do you have some crazy room decorations? Challenge them to a room decoration competition. Bet them that your decorations are better. If they're vibing, they'll accept the challenge and come to your room to check out your digs. You should be able to get the rest from there. Maybe make up a puppy or a kitten that they can come see, and then try to play it off when it isn't there. Or buy a bunny rabbit. They'll want to pet that.

*pong is not foreplay, and do not drink if you're under 21

"Flitzing"

A Neophyte's Guide

"Flitzing" derives its name from an unsubtle combination of the words "flirt" and "blitzing". It is, in its simplest form, the act of flirting over blitz. But it's so much more than that. For many, it's a way of life. For others, it's just a way to pass the time.

The first step in flitzing is having somebody to flitz with. This could be that girl you accidentally spilled a beer on last night or that cute guy in your EARS class. Doesn't matter who it is, so long as you know them at least a little, are interested, and have something to start a conversation on. You can't blitz a random person, and you can't just say, "Hey, what's up?" No need to be boring or a sketchball.

Before we go on with the other steps of flitzing, there are some style points that need to be addressed.

a. Don't capitalize anything in your flitzes. Punctuation is to be used at your discretion. But don't be that person with the semi-colon. Nobody wants to f*ck the guy with the semi-colon.

b. Don't sign off with your name, or with anything at all. "Best, Lawrence" is how you sign off to a professor, not a potential squeeze.

c. The subject line should not actually be the subject of the blitz. Instead, it should be the start of the first sentence. For example: "Subject: I had" "Message: no idea that our professor has been bringing his cat to class. That's unreal!"

So with that in mind, you now have to write the opening flitz. Keep it casual. It shouldn't be too long. It should be funny. And it should have the potential for response. There are two ways to do this. The first is to have it be so outrageously funny that they have to respond. The second is to include a question at some point that they can answer.

This brings us to another point: all good flitzes should have the potential for response. If you send a flitz that doesn't have potential for response, that's bad. The feeling of reading one of those flitzes is the exact same feeling as when your dog kills a squirrel in the backyard and brings it to your feet as a prize. I mean, that's great and everything, but what am I supposed to do with that?

Once you've got the conversation going, the only thing to do is to make sure you don't seem overeager. Flitzing is a give-and-take. Don't respond immediately. Just like in the movie *Swingers*, where you wait two days before you call a girl, you have to wait a little while to respond to a flitz. Can't seem desperate. A good rule of thumb is to wait the same amount of time that the other person waits. Five minutes? An hour? Three days? Six days? Whatever.

The last step is to segue this digital flirtation into some physical intimacy. There are two avenues you can choose for this. The first is the "Hey, maybe I'll see you at TDX later" approach, where you make a point to meet up at a frat later and then hopefully head home together. If this works, good for you. But don't expect every girl to fall for this. Some need a little in-person wooing.

For in-person wooing, you have tons of choice. If you're a complete n00b, you can ask to play a game of pong with a girl. If you're a partial n00b, you can ask to watch a movie. If you're a chotch, you can invite them to Canoe Club for dinner. If you're the man, you can invite a girl to go on a bowl-and-bowl with you, which is where you smoke a bowl and then go bowling. Use your imagination. People like having fun more than not having fun.

Well, that's it. Apple+M.

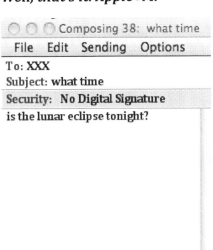

SOCIAL LIFE

The Dartmouth Seven

Tide Detergent - Available at Topside

To put it simply, the Dartmouth Seven is a list of seven public places you're supposed to have sex before you graduate. But it's really much more than that. It's the litmus test for having the true college experience. **If you graduate with all seven under your belt, then that's better than graduating summa cum laude.** The most difficult part of doing the Seven is finding somebody to do it with (duh). Once you do that, it's easy-peasey, lemon-squeezey.

1. Stacks

Stacks is the iconic one of the Seven. It's by far the easiest, too. It's indoor, so you can do it during any term, and it's secluded, so it requires no planning. Just turn to the person studying next to you and ask if they want to take a trip into the stacks with you. Actually, don't do that. Keep it classy. Remember to put the condom wrapper into a random book afterwards.

2. BEMA

The BEMA is the cop-out on the list. It's just silly. It's outdoors, but not cool at all, since nobody ever goes to the BEMA. You just kinda do it and then it's done. Umm...

3. Center of the Green

This one's pretty sweet. No matter what time of night you do, somebody's definitely gonna be walking by, and an S&S car driving by just might see you. This is the peak of exhibitionism. Shave your ass before you do it, bro.

4. President's Lawn

Easily the most badass of the Seven. You're fornicating on the President's Lawn! If he wakes up and looks out his window, he'll see you and your mate going to Humplebees. When you shake the President's hand at graduation, you can tell him/her, "Thanks for the free parking." Classic.

5. Steps of Dartmouth Hall

This one's tricky. For a lot of reasons. The first is that you're supposed to have sex on stone steps, and that means somebody's getting a cold butt, and both of you are probably going to get some scrapes. Oh well. Also, the front of Dartmouth Hall is lit up until around 4:30 a.m., so you'll have to do it in between then and dawn. Timing, timing.

6. Top of the Hop

Find a Studio Art major, borrow their ID card, go into The Hop really late at night, and bang it out in the Top of the Hop while you watch the sun rise over the Green. That's heaven.

7. 50-yard line

I guess people used to care a lot about football, so that's why we have this one.

8. (Bonus) Bartlett Tower

Bartlett Tower is no longer one of the official seven, but if you can manage to get in, you absolutely must take advantage of that and tell me how it went. I've always dreamed.

*looking for a book on the bottom shelf - certainly not the Bible

Top 10 Places to Poop

Do the right thing

1. East Asia Bathroom:

This is the holy grail of poopholes in the library. Go to the East Asian Studies room in the stacks and head to the left. Go through a door. On your left is a door marked "Private". The lighting is soft, the lock on the door is secure, and the solitude is complete. Enjoy. Bring a magazine, or bring a smartphone and catch up on your tweets.

2. Collis Second Floor Men's Bathroom:

There aren't that many men in Collis, and almost none of the men make it up to the second floor. This bathroom is recently renovated and rarely trafficked. Modern toilets just feel different under the cheeks.

3. East Wheelock Hall Bathrooms:

Apparently the East Wheelock people were trying some sociological experiment when they designed these bathrooms. The toilets and showers are in these little individual rooms in the dorm hallways that look like closets. The sinks are in the hallway. So you have to poop in a closet and then brush your teeth with poop-covered hands in the hallway. F*ckin' weird, man.

4. Parkhurst Basement:

People tend to shit their pants getting Parkhursted in the basement, but few actually make it to the dungeon bathroom. It's lit by torches and has gargoyles that watch you while you drop your dookie.

5. Hanover Inn Basement Bathroom:

You'll probably end up here by accident. It'll blow your mind. The Hanover Inn itself is old and feels slightly dusty no matter how clean it is. The bathroom in the basement is polished and sparkling and I feel like my poop is going to be tastefully lemon-scented.

6. Brothers/Sisters-only bathrooms of Greek Houses:

Many frat and sorority houses have bathrooms that are for members only. Not only are these bathrooms treated with a much higher degree of respect than the other bathrooms in the house, but they also develop interesting personalities and tend to have truly phenomenal reading lists. Feel the collective butt-warmth of your brother/sisterhood.

7. Stinson's:

I dare you to find the bidet in Stinson's and use it.

8. Reserves Single Bathroom, Wheeler-side:

Similar to the East Asia Bathroom, but not quite as good. Use it when the East Asia Bathroom is occupied.

9. Port-a-Potties at construction sites on campus:

The weird looks you'll get coming out of that thing totally validate the smell and the lack of view besides illuminated green plastic with the shadow of the neighboring Port-a-Potty on it.

10. Women's Handicapped Stall in the Midfay Basement:

Since half of each sophomore class lives in the Fayerweathers (unconfirmed), you'll definitely end up in here at some point. It's great for showers, great for pooping, great for phone conversations, great for having sex in. This thing isn't a bathroom. It's a room. That happens to have bathroom stuff in it. Spread out in here and enjoy whatever it is you're doing. Even if you don't live here, make a point to stop by with that special someone on your way home from AD/Heorot.

Heckling

Insight for the sake of insight...

Ah, the fine art of heckling. Whether you are just a casual sports fan or a face-painting, sign-making, slurrer of the alma mater, there is no denying that a good heckler can make spectating a pleasure even if The Big Green is losing. There are wits aplenty at Dartmouth, where students are smart enough to be in the Ivy League and were cool enough in high school to know that popping your collar and being in an a cappella group don't boost your social capital (read: Harvard, Yale, and Princeton). Much to the disdain of some uptight members of the Upper Valley community, namely a certain Valley News sports reporter, there is no shortage of cunning linguists at this fine institution, making Dartmouth a very difficult place to play as an opposing player. Although a JV heckler might believe this task to be as easy as showing up and being loud or crude, a varsity heckler knows that unlike 'Nam there are certain rules to follow to be awesome, but also to ensure you don't end up in 'cuffs or as a national headline.

Alcohol helps

Alcohol and sports go hand in hand. Alcohol and Dartmouth go hand in hand. Unfortunately the transitive property is not at work here because most of our sports teams suck. Damn. Good thing God gave us this inhibition-eliminating potion because life's not fair and alcohol makes it bearable. Yeah, yeah, some people might say that you don't need to drink to have fun but why use two sticks to make a fire when you have lighters? Alcohol makes life, and people, funnier. You're a shitty heckler if you're not drunk, I promise. Alcohol is the steroids of heckling, and much like in the MLB where everyone's using steroids, you're going to suck if you're not. But too much alcohol, like too many steroids, (read: Barry Bonds) gets you in trouble.

Use Facebook

We live in a day and age where people's skeletons are no longer in their closet; they are on the Internet. You'd be a fool if you didn't do a simple Facebook search to find out that their best player "wishes there was a 'love-it' button." The dirt is there, my friend - dig it up.

Foreigners are target #1

Much like in middle school dodge ball where the first rule of combat is to gang up on the scrawny-armed, glasses-wearing, pale kid who sits on a bench by himself at recess, the easiest target in heckling is the foreign kid with a mullet and earrings. He is the easiest target not only because it's still cool to wear chokers in Europe but also because despite having just bageled our best player, a crowd-igniting "U-S-A" chant is a reminder that freedom is a dish best served in our country and not in theirs.

Don't heckle girls

I know, I know, its really tempting but don't. It's a lose-lose. If you're a good heckler you will most likely find some up-tight dad's fist in your face, and girls won't hook up with you because you're an asshole. If you're a bad heckler you'll get that same dad's fist in your face, and girls wont hook up with you because you're not funny.

*"#22, your shorts are on backwards, you pathetic loser"

SOCIAL LIFE

Not Going Greek?

Whatever.

You might have the impression that Dartmouth is dominated by Greek life. Well, not too far from the mark. But that doesn't mean you need to join a house in order to take advantage of the social scene. In fact, for the right person, staying a free agent might be one of the best decisions you make.

As far as organized social activities go, the Greek houses pretty much run the show. You'll get meetings once a week, formals at some fancy country club, various mixers with persons of the opposite or same gender, and naked games of Mario Tennis.

But as a free agent (I prefer that term to the unnecessarily serious "unaffiliated," which sounds like something you'd tell a census bureau, and "GDI," which sounds like an intestinal parasite my friends caught in Costa Rica), you can piggyback on some of the scene-creating legwork done by your fratty brethren (and sororry sistren) while maintaining your freedom to do your own thing, too. I'll explain this strategy as a geometrical formula:

a. Greek house plans scene.
b. Greek house extends invitations for people to attend scene.
c. You attend scene with complete disregard for Step B.
d. Fun is had.
e. Greek house pays for scene/cleans up scene/gets on each other's nerves after scene/receives ire from various forces within the administration and reactionary Upper Valley circles for having scene. You leave.
f. Do something else.

Q.E.D.

Greek houses provide you with a social safety net, and for many people, that's really important. But not having that safety net, while perhaps a bit scarier at first, can be even more rewarding in the long run. You have to make your own way. You have to try a little harder to plan activities, try a little harder to make friends, and try a little harder to find a TV so you can watch SportsCenter in your boxers. But if you make it to the other side in one piece, it's worth it.

For one, having some added flexibility with your time gives you the opportunity to do a pretty wide range of activities. If you don't have to clean the basement Thursday afternoon, you might spend the day hiking Moosilauke instead, or exploring the area. If you're not busy handing out wristbands and pretending to care who gets them, then maybe you'll go see a show at The Hop, take a trip to Montreal, or visit your friend's art gallery. There are a lot of things to do in Hanover, believe it or not, and a lot of people graduate with regrets at not taking advantage of a broader variety. Don't be one of them.

Second, this one's for the guys, you won't get as fat. Seriously. No need to get on the midlife beer belly train before you have to.

Third, if you're not in a house, people can't pigeonhole you as easily. At Dartmouth, people often rely on quick soundbites to determine what kind of person you are, and Greek houses are the most frequent and totalizing identifier. Oh, you're in that house? Must be a druggie. You pledged where? Guess you're a misogynist. House identities are hardly set in stone, but once you join one, you may wind up with a few rivalries or latent hostilities you didn't sign up for. Telling people you're not in a house provokes a reaction, too, but it's usually just one of honest puzzlement. Have confidence to be yourself, barrel through it, and everything will be fine. Honestly, having the confidence to do your own thing might be the single most important thing you can do socially at Dartmouth. **People stereotype here, but the people that really flourish are the ones that push right past it.**

So, then, how do you replace the social safety net of a Greek house? Lots of ways:

1. Friends are everywhere. Classes, organizations, the gym, the Green, the sauna. Say hi. There are lots of places that people hang out that aren't frat basements, and these are the places you make lots of your lasting friendships, anyway. Sports games. Collis porch. That heat vent thing across from Topliff. This gets easier over time, as you get to know your class, but don't be afraid to just talk to people. Create your own scenes. Just do things. Jump in.

2. Find other groups. Even the most ardent free agents need fallback groups sometimes, so pick ones that make it easy for you. Performance groups (a cappella, improv, dance), sports (varsity, club, intramurals), publications (liberal, conservative, Freemason), roommates, spontaneous secret societies, book clubs. You know. Whatever gets you from A to B.

3. Frats are your friends. See aforementioned geometric proof.

4. Date date date date date date. People say it doesn't happen at Dartmouth. Ignore them. Find a partner in crime, go on adventures.

5. Bring the social scene to you. Rent a sweet off-campus house or apartment, or turn your dorm into Hanover's coolest pad. Get a TV, rent some couches, build a bar, decorate. C'mon. Decorating's cool. Seriously, guys.

With a little effort, you can build your own social groups exactly how you want them, be friendly with as broad a cross-section of campus as you can stomach and still hang out at Chi Gam all you want.

At the end of the day, just remember that the most important social developments in college don't have anything to do with others. They have to do with you. John Wooden, UCLA's legendary basketball coach, used to say, "Be more concerned with your character than your reputation." That couldn't be wiser. Be true to yourself, be good to others. The rest will follow.

-Jamie Berk, Free Agent, Class of 2011

Overheards

{ Because **Seniors** say the darn'dest things! }

"F*CK CAREER SERVICES"

SENIOR #1: "DUDE, CAN I GET ANOTHER PAIR OF SENIOR SUNGLASSES?"
SENIOR GEAR CHAIR: "UM, WHY?"
SENIOR #1: "I BROKE MINE DANCING AT C+G FORMAL, C'MON!"

{ SENIOR GIRL: "I SERIOUSLY DON'T KNOW HOW I CAN JUSTIFY HOOKING UP WITH SOMEONE WHO CAN'T LEARN TO HIGHLIGHT THEIR BLITZES." }

FROSH GIRL: "SO WHAT ARE YOU DOING NEXT YEAR?"
SENIOR GUY: "I'M WORKING FOR THE PEACE CORPS IN UGANDA ACTUALLY."
FROSH GIRL: "OMG REALLY?!"
SENIOR GUY (LAUGHING): "NO, I'M DOING INVESTMENT BANKING IN NYC."

SENIOR #1 (NOSTALGICALLY): "I CAN'T BELIEVE THIS IS MY LAST GAME OF PONG AT ALPHA CHI!"
SENIOR #2: "ISN'T THIS YOUR FIRST?"
SENIOR #1: "YEA...SO?"

{ "I WOKE UP THIS MORNING ON MY FRESHMAN FLOOR. LIKE ACTUALLY ON THE FLOOR" }

SOCIAL LIFE

Dartmouth Outing Club
"The DOC"

The Dartmouth Outing Club (DOC) is the oldest and largest collegiate outdoors club in the country. It is made up of a handful of sub-clubs, each focused on a different activity.

While these clubs at times seem insular and difficult to get involved with casually, almost all of them offer beginners and other public trips, though these trips are usually not well publicized. It's worth getting in touch with a club if you're interested in trying out what they do.

Dartmouth Mountaineering Club (DMC)

This sub-club is for anyone who loved to climb trees and subsequently break limbs when they were younger. Bring out the inner adrenaline junkie in yourself and join trips ranging from beginner bouldering to ice climbing.

Mountain Biking Club

Self explanatory.

*view of the White Mountains from the River Dorms

Bait and Bullet

Like shootin' shit? Like catchin' shit? Like catchin' then shootin' shit? Then you'll love this sub-club! B&B organizes huntin' and fishin' trips all year round and also maintains the Dartmouth Shooting Range, which you can access for free to let out some post-finals stress.

Ledyard Canoe Club

If you like kayaking or canoeing, join this club. This will come in handy during sophomore summer when Cerberus at the front desk will charge you $15 at all costs to use a water vehicle. Don't try and rent one without paying. You. Will. Get. Caught.

Dartmouth Ski Patrol

The closest thing to a cult on Dartmouth campus. Kidding... sort of. Members of this club are selected during an über-competitive process freshman year, which gives the upperclassmen ample time to warp their brains and feed them the punch when they are ripe. If you plan on spending all four winters at Dartmouth (you crazy!) and love skiing, then this is the club for you.

Organic Farm

The people that operate this farm are the nicest and most welcoming on campus. Their carrots would make Bugs Bunny an addict and provide the average human with night vision after only two bites.

Cabin and Trail

Maintains fifty miles of the Appalachian Trail stretching from Hanover to Mt. Moosilauke (the stretch covered by the biannual "50" hike). Also operates the DOC Cabins in this corridor. If you don't understand their name at this point... f*ck you.

Getting Outside

Get Crunchy

Besides trips run by DOC Clubs, there are tons of hikes and outdoors spots in the Upper Valley worth exploring on your own. Here are some of the best, all within a thirty minute drive of Hanover. You're missing out on a big part of what Dartmouth has to offer if you don't make it to at least a few of these places in your four years here.

Mt. Cardigan

Considering how close it is to Hanover, how short the walk is, and how incredible the views are, Cardigan is the best hike in the Upper Valley. It's also the most overlooked (get it?). The top of the peak was cleared by forest fire, and is now a huge rock clearing that offers incredibly scenic views conducive to many activities... **many activities.**

Directions: It's a thirty minute drive to the trailhead, and then 1.5 miles hike up to the summit. Take I-89 South one exit to Route 4 East (exit 17). After about twelve miles, turn left onto Route 118 North. Take a right at the Canaan Speedway, and follow that road to the Cardigan parking lot.

The Ledges

The Ledges are the **go-to swimming hole outside of Hanover.** After parking in a poorly marked lot, stumbling down a very-steep hill, and nearly breaking your ankle on some slippery rocks, you will arrive at The Ledges, with pools for swimming, and waterfalls for falling.

Directions: Take Route 10 (Main Street) South out of town to West Leb, and turn onto 12A south ("the strip" in West Leb). Go past all of the shopping centers in West Leb and continue south on that road. A bit further down, turn left onto Trues Brook Road, and park at the parking area about a miles down. The Ledges are a short walk down the trail from the parking area.

Union Village Dam

Navigating this labyrinth of a national park is tough, but rewarding when you find the right swimming spot. If you're feeling alternative, up for an adventure, or like things blocking surges of liquid at a high velocity, then this place is for you.

Directions: Cross the Ledyard Bridge and drive through Norwich. Continue straight on the main road that passes through Norwich (which turns into Union Village Road) for about five miles, then turn left on Route 132 West. After a half mile, turn right onto Academy Road, where there's a sign for Union Village Dam. You can take Route 5 to Route 132.

Balch Hill

Where the GREEN editors inadvertently met for the first time during the DOC sponsored picnic-by-yourself day, Balch Hill has solidified itself as the **top first-makeout spot in Hanover.** Watching the sunset on this scenic hill is second to none, so bring a significant other, a date, or a pet to keep you company during one of nature's most beautiful recurring events.

Directions: Take East Wheelock Street out of town (past Kappa and A-Lot). Park in the lot where Grasse Road veers off to the left, after about 1.5 miles. The trail up to Balch Hill is just across the street from the parking lot. The walk up takes less than ten minutes.

Gile Mountain/Fire Tower

Located down a dirt road in Norwich, the Fire Tower has great views of the Upper Valley. Smoke here.

Directions: Cross the Ledyard Bridge and drive through Norwich. Just on the other side of downtown, turn left onto Turnpike Road. Stay left where the road forks, and then keep staying straight (for a long time) as the road turns to dirt and gets more narrow. Park on the left and walk up.

DOC Cabins

Notable cabins include Hinman and Armington, both of which are twenty - thirty minutes away and located on lakes with canoes. The massive, newly rebuilt Harris Cabin on Moose Mountain can sleep fifty and is only a ten minute drive from campus. Nunnemacher, located on the Dartmouth Skiway, can be skied to in winter or hiked to in summer. Billings Lodge Cabin in Randolph, NH has electricity and running water and is an awesome base for exploring the White Mountains (being fifteen minutes drive from Mt. Washington and directly across the street from the Mt. Adams trailhead). Visit the DOC website to rent a cabin.

VII

Dining

"To make people happy, that is what cooking is about."

Aunt Jemima, 1993

Dartmouth Dining Services

An Overview of "DDS"

We seniors are certainly sad to leave the school that we've all come to love over these four years. It truly is our home from home. Our nostalgia is suitably quoted in the traditional Dartmouth tune, "Dartmouth Undying":

Who can forget her sharp and misty mornings, the clanging bells, the crush of feet on snow. Her sparkling noons, the crowding into Commons, the long white afternoons, the twighlight glows?

The friends we've made are eternal, and the professors have been true mentors. [Somebody keep saying nostalgic things, I'm bad at this] _____.

Each of these things that we will dearly miss are unquestionably outweighed by the prospect that we will never have to eat DDS again. And to be perfectly honest, we're leaving DDS at its prime—the future certainly looks grim.

*Homeplate, we will miss you

Food Court

"The Class of 1953 Commons"

You'll quickly find that Dartmouth has tried to change the name of Thayer Hall to The Class of 1953 Commons. Not that we even know who Thayer is, really, but why have we ditched his name? Even '53 alums don't like the change—it's too long and doesn't make sense. I suppose Homeplate wasn't baseball themed, but even the Arnold Schwarzenegger Stadium in Sturm Graz, Austria still has the word stadium in it. Just call it the Dining Hall, or something along those lines, please. Before the Class of '53 butted in, here is some relevant advice.

Try to Avoid Primetime:

Primetime, as you could imagine, is when Food Court turns from a barren wasteland into a barren wasteland swarming with freshmen. While all Kappas and KDE's disagree, there are times in the day where minimal facetime is allowable. If you want any chance of ordering anything but the sesame-crusted tilapia, take this advice. Avoid primetime. Lunch primetime strikes after any class gets out. Solution? Don't take class. Dinner primetime is from 6 to 7:30. Eat early, eat late, or don't eat.

It's Not a Walkway, It's a Runway:

We're not talking about planes here. But rather that the FoCo walkway is a continual amateur-modeling exhibition. At primetime there's no less than three hundred people watching prospective pong dates come and go. This is no place to spill a drink and it's certainly no place to fall (see: Model Falls Twice on youtube). For guys eating, it's their chance to be fashion judges but still seem cool: *"Jessica is looking hot today."* For girls, the runway is fodder for small talk when all else has failed: *"OMG did you see that guy?"/"Yeah."/"Yeah, me too."*

Froyo Does Not Mean Fat-Free:

It means frozen-yogurt. Remember this one. That is all.

DINING

Good Now Doesn't Mean Good Later:

There's really nothing you can do to both satisfy your appetite and save your digestive system.

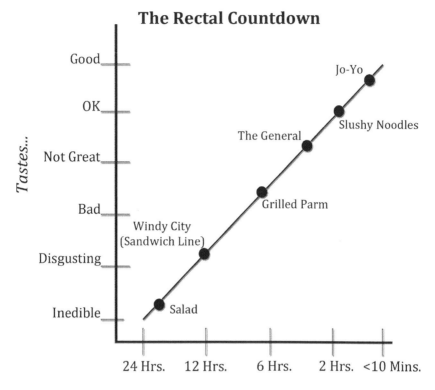

As you can see, the y-axis shows a scale of how good your meal tastes, and the x-axis is your rectal countdown. Based on pure science, the better something tastes, the quicker you will have diarrhea. If you learn anything from this chart, have it be that irregular deposits will occur in a maximum window of 24-hour periods. And this is no savings bank, people. What does this mean? Well, unless you can bear pooping in a public bathroom, you're going to wish that your room was closer to Food Court. You'll drop your tray and run faster than a Kenyan in mile 25. **If you think that's racist then you're racist.**

Collis

"The Collis Center For Student Involvement"

Collis, officially titled "The Collis Center For Student Involvement," was constructed in 1973 as an alternative to The Hop for alternative people. The fraternity-hating types were forever unleashed from the depths of the Hopkins Center and given smoothies and pastries.

Everyone knows that FoCo gives you your thirty seconds of fame on the way to the froyo machine. **Collis dwellers don't have that aggressive "be seen" mentality**. I mean, they do, but instead of being seen on the red carpet it's more like "Oh no, the cameras accidentally caught me at a Charity Fundraiser for Blind Seeing Eye Dogs. I swear it wasn't on purpose."

If you think that you're going to eat lunch at Collis in between classes, think again. The stir-fry line is longer than an anaconda, and girls clog the pastry aisle like a breakfast bomb does a toilet. But if you manage to sneak in between classes, the omelets and stir-fry are top class, relatively speaking, of course. If your conscience can bear cutting a thirty-minute line, you can even **get "Collis Pasta" for dinner, which is sure to give you a satisfying meal** - just don't look at the price.

Counterintuitively, Late Night Collis is like alternative-person repellant. Pretend-reading and small salads are replaced with chicken tenders and Americanized sushi-rolls starting at 9:30 p.m., Sunday - Thursday. This is the perfect time to get your nightly fix of complaining about your Econ problem set to your friends while trying to get noticed by senior guys and girls.

The Hop

"The Courtyard Cafe"

In attempting to name this page, I have learned that The Courtyard Café is the actual name of what we students call "The Hop". Not that it's a bad name—I mean there is actually a courtyard in The Hop, believe it or not—but from here on out we refer to it strictly as "The Hop".

The Hop is great—plain and simple. For no apparent reason, apart from amusement, imagine every DDS institution as a different kind of dog. If Collis is a Poodle and Food Court is a Finnish Hound, The Hop is a Golden Retriever. It's loyal and it's always there for you. It doesn't close at awkward hours of the day and doesn't judge you when you're eating your first meal at 3:30 in the afternoon—even if you're eating a breakfast bomb and sipping on a 32 oz. Cherry Coke. It lets you make up your own orders like the PLM (next page), which we thought was close enough to teaching your Golden Retriever new tricks. The Hop doesn't bark at you or shed too much, and it doesn't get fleas. We can end the dog comparison right there.

Since it's not as easy to criticize The Hop, we've decided to give you a list of its commonly eaten meals for your convenience (we've added some "Senior Plays"). We've written them down exactly as you should order them, so that people don't hate you for holding up the line.

Breakfast/Lunch:

Legend has it that if you make it to The Hop before 11 a.m. you can order waffles, omelets, and French toast. So you've slept through your 2a. Food Court is closed and Collis is for pussies. Nobody likes cats.

Bacon, Egg & Cheese
How to order: "Bacon breakfast bagel, please."
Tastiness: Very
Mandatory: Frank's Red Hot

The Lyman Missimer
How to order: "Steak breakfast, two eggs, onions, wheat toast, please."
Height: 5' 11
First/Middle Names: 0

The PLM
How to order: "3 eggs over medium, side of ham & tomatoes, 2 toasted English muffins, please."
Delicious?: Delicious
Mandatory: Fork and knife to mix it all together

Dinner:

Both Collis and Food Court are naturally packed and you need to get some grease in your system. The Hop serves eggs all day. If you're sick of eggs, somehow, here's what you can get for dinner to change it up:

General Tso's Chicken
How to order: "The General, please."
Presentation: Simple, elegant
Chopsticks: Optional

BBQ Bacon Cheeseburger
How to order: "Big Bad Burger, please."
Patty: Huge, delicious
Rectal Countdown: 45 mins

Chicken Tender Quesadilla
How to order: "Tender queso, please."
*The DDS staff spells it "caso"...

Hanover Restaurants

The Melting Pot

Bagel Basement

When you are in the need for an unbelievable, crispy-on-the-outside, soft-on-the-inside bagel, the authors recommend H+H bagels in the Upper East Side. But, if the line at The Hop has wrapped back to the mailboxes, and nursing your hangover is your top priority, calling a Bagel Basement audible quickly becomes a reality. No one cares that you used to go to this place in the city that had the best schmear you've ever tasted; in case you forgot, we're in Hanover.

Bagel Basement has a **variety of decent bagels that are more than enjoyable** for a college student's delicate palate. Their entire menu is written out completely in chalk on the back wall. You're not Alan Richman, so stop complaining and go take care of your Sunday morning hangover with some bagels.

Recommended Dish: The Famous #2, $6.25

Boloco

I think one day a Chipotle came to Hanover, had an identity crisis, and is now cross-dressing as Boloco. While their slogan claims they are in the business of "inspired burritos," I have no idea what that means. If you are looking for a bean-cheese-and-meat Mexican burrito, you should probably go to Gusanoz. That being said, Boloco's unique "burrito" options allow you to avoid the painful after effects of the Habanero (see: Gusanoz).

Their menu consists of "alternative" burritos like the Buffalo, Summer, and Caesar, which are all made well and taste fine. With a plethora of options, all of which can also be eaten in bowl form, **Boloco has a burrito for anyone's picky appetite.** Some may complain about quality, but honestly, it is no worse than anywhere else. **Boloco also** offers a variety of shakes; the best of which is the peanut butter and banana flavored Jimmy Carter. In case you wanted to order delivery, Boloco is well known to take a comically long time to get its food to students, especially during finals, so be prepared to wait.

Recommended Dish: Caesar Wrap $6.25; Summer Burrito $6.25

C&A Pizza

A book could be written about the rumors that circulate about C&A Pizza or "C&A's". In full disclosure, I don't know who actually eats at C&A's, and come to think of it I don't even know who actually orders from there either – it's unclear how C&A's stays in business. About once every two terms, one of your friends will ask you mid-pong game, "Hey, want to order C&A's?" and once the two of you get past the "isn't that place a front?" conversation, you will finally agree to order some pizza and grinders – the only rule: only delivery, never live.

The **pizzas are greasier than EBA's (see EBA's), but they are unquestionably better**, especially while drunk. It isn't hard to understand why the thick, greasy pizzas that haven't changed for years have been consumed by drunk Dartmouth students for generations (including a parent of one of the authors). The **unknown gem on the C&A's menu, however, is the grinder**. Even if the thought of hamburger grinder sounds unappetizing, try it before you knock it. The authors recommend either the hamburger or the meatball grinders, both of which come warm and are the perfect post-game meals. And honestly, after a few games of pong, what else do you need?

Recommended Dish: Large Pepperoni Pizza, $11.45; Hamburger Grinder, $5.95; Meatball Grinder, $5.95

Canoe Club

The Canoe Club is the nicest restaurant in Hanover, reserved for either special events or when your parents are in town – think live music and a magician that does tricks tableside. But then again given the fact that we are in Hanover, it's more Benihana-on-your-sister's-birthday nice than country club nice. With that said, the Canoe Club **has some great dishes, especially relative to the other restaurants in the Hanover area.**

The Canoe Club Cheeseburger has peppers and onions

incorporated into local meat imported from Vermont. The grilled capicola ham and Swiss cheese sandwich on the late night menu is also an honorable mention. But **every time I go, whether or not I am hungry, I order their take on moules marinières – two dozen New England mussels**, sautéed in garlic, lemon, and white wine, served marinating in their own flavorful broth, and covered in a sheet of crispy fries and garlic aioli. Whether you are eating the mussels one by one, or dipping the fries in the garlic-mussel-aioli juice that is left behind, the combination of textures and flavors leaves you hanging onto every bite.

The Canoe Club bar (which actually has a very impressive selection of scotch) is a weekend hot spot for Dartmouth grad students; so if you are a senior girl who has declared herself a MRS major, stop by to see if you can find "true love" between martinis with a Tuck student trying to relive the city life at the bar.

Recommended Dish: *Rope Cultured Mussels and Fries, $13.00; Canoe Club Cheeseburger, $11.00*

Dirt Cowboy Café

The only real coffee shop in the area, Dirt Cowboy has been feeding the addictions of New York girls for years. Situated at the top of Main Street, stroll in and find yourself packed into the smallest ordering area imaginable. If you can somehow navigate yourself to the front of the line, you finally have earned the right to **choose from what seems like hundreds of gourmet coffees and teas.** Their selection is actually good, and the seating area, although small, usually has a spot where you can sit and talk or get work done (like writing a book).

Dirt Cowboy sandwiches are limited in variety, and the meat and cheese won't change your worldview, but the Fox Hollow Farm Sweet & Spicy Vermont mustard that comes with them is unbelievably delicious and pairs well with your iced chai.

Recommended Dish: *Cream Earl Gray Tea, $3.25; Salami and Cheese sandwich, $5.00*

Everything But Anchovies (EBA's)

If there is one truth this book can claim, it is that you will eat something from EBA's before you finish reading this sentence. Just finished a game of pong? Need fifteen pizzas for that student group? **The food, to put it bluntly, is bad**. Everything is fried, mediocre at best, and your heart sort of hurts after your meal, but nothing compares to a buffalo chicken ("buff-chick") pizza after your fourth game.

The menu is extensive: burgers, chicken sandwiches, tenders, pizza, salads, Tuscany bread – whatever you could want when drunk or high. But **the main reason EBA's will be a staple for the foreseeable future is not the food, it's the delivery times**. You will quickly realize that every food option in Hanover closes at midnight, and unless you are a loser, you should be hanging out until 2 a.m. – EBA's saw the arbitrage opportunity and started delivering until 2:10 a.m.

There is very little reason to actually go to EBA's (unless you get invited to Kappa Semi), so on any given Friday or Saturday, I would guess that 20% of campus is trying to get through the phone lines at 2:09 a.m., and be warned, they won't accept a single order past 2:10 a.m. While the 2:09 order is a right of passage for most Dartmouth students, your student body asks you to do it only under the most extreme conditions. (603) 643-6135, just program it into your phone now.

Recommended Dish: Large Buffalo Chicken pizza, $15.49; Southern Style Chicken Tender Basket, $9.59

Gusanoz

Let's get this out of the way, you are going to feel like shit after you eat at Gusanoz. Even with their inevitable gastrointestinal problems, Gusanoz has become Hanover's premier "Mexican" restaurant. While the competition (Boloco) may not put up much of a fight, Gusanoz **offers a variety of "traditional" Mexican dishes – burritos, tacos, tortas, and quesadillas**. Sure, the rice is a little mushy and the beans are undercooked, but for the love of God, stop complaining – the nearest Chipotle is 97.4 miles away. Get over yourself.

Be aware, however, the extra-spicy Habanero Burrito is nearly inedible, and you will be feeling its after-effects for days. Recently, Gusanoz participated in a hostile take over of the Ben and Jerry's Ice Cream Shop next door and spun out its own leveraged ice cream division that offers Walpole (a b-side Ben and Jerry's). Talk about synergies.

Finally, Gusanoz has a secret weapon that overshadows their average selection of Mexican food and misplaced ice cream, and his name is **Jim Gusanoz.** Jim Real-Last-Name-Unknown is the delivery guy, and is genuinely one of the nicest people I have ever met. Every frat on campus thinks they have a special relationship with him, every person has their own Jim Gusanoz anecdote, and there isn't a soul on campus who doesn't like him. Whether you do Gusanoz live or order delivery, get your friends, buy some Tums, and say hi to Jim for me.

Recommended Dish: Burrito Especial, $6.99; Carne Asada tortas, $4.99

Jewel of India

There are few things more rogue than doing Jewel live. Going to the seemingly completely out of place Indian restaurant on the outskirts of town (read: 2 minutes away), is an event in itself, but given that delivery often takes over an hour, and that sometimes they simply say they "don't deliver," doing it live is often your only choice. Jewel is **the most authentic ethnic restaurant in Hanover**, and that's probably because actual Indian people run the place. Regardless, **the food, while heavy, is actually very good**.

The curries are flavorful, the naan is soft, and the rice is fluffy. An ideal meal would consist of a few close friends sharing various curries and naans family style so that everyone can try each of the intensely spiced meals. For beginners, the authors recommend sticking with the creamy, tomato-based chicken tikka masala. If you feel ready to venture past novice, two great options are the lamb vindaloo and the vegetarian saag paneer.

Finally, each customer has the option of personalizing the spice level of his or her dish. From personal experience, it's unclear if the waiter actually listens to you or just stereotypes, but "extra spicy" is never that spicy. The wait staff often times comes off as extremely disgruntled, but I think its because something is lost in translation. As long as you're not on a date, Jewel is a perfect spot to head with a group of friends for an off-night dinner that will more than fill you up.

Recommended Dish: Chicken Tikka Masala, $12.95; Lamb Vindaloo, $11.95; Saag Paneer, $10.95

Lou's

Lou's is the zenith of Dartmouth dining, not in terms of the food, but because it's an experience every Dartmouth student should have. While on face Lou's is just a diner that opens early, it has been in the same location on Main Street since 1947 (and has pictures on the walls spanning every era since).

In terms of the cuisine, the gigantic "Big Green" breakfast is a common order – two buttermilk pancakes, two slices of French toast, two eggs, bacon, sausage, homefries, and your choice of toast. But the tenured customers know that the **poached eggs and corned beef hash are exquisite**. Cooked well, not overly salted, and hearty, the hash is the way to go. Finally, if you can force another bite, have one of Lou's freshly baked **"mile-high" pies – famously delicious**. Supposedly, a lunch menu exists, and I've been told that something on it is pretty good, but stick to breakfast.

Before you graduate make sure you experience going to Lou's on a Saturday or Sunday morning, waiting in the forty-five-minute line, and sitting at a table too small for the amount of food you ordered. Second, for the hard guys, try to play pong until Lou's opens at 7:00 a.m., order, and try not to fall asleep before your hash comes. Lou's hasn't changed in years and won't anytime soon, so when you get the chance, get your friends together and go order the hash – Lest the old traditions fail.

Recommended Dish: *Poached Eggs and Corned Beef Hash, $8.95; The Big Green, $10.25*

Mai Thai

I've had Mai Thai less than a half-dozen times in my career at Dartmouth. The one time I went there live, the service was abysmal, and the few times that I ordered delivery, I've been extremely under whelmed. Let's start with the curry. When I order Thai green curry, I differentiate based on nuance. Hints of chili, lime leaf, galangal, and coriander should shine through while the creamy fullness of the coconut milk fills out the base.

Now I know you are thinking, "But GREEN, don't you hate it when people are overly critical of ethnic foods in Hanover?" Yes, but **Mai Thai isn't even trying**. The **curry is flavorless, the sticky rice tastes like rice-a-roni**, and the chicken is dryer than a Math 8 lecture. The Pad Thai is too slippery, tasteless, and the meat is never cooked well. I would give Mai Thai some leeway if they actually tried once and a while, instead every time I order, I leave disappointed and wishing I ordered something else. Hey Mai Thai, you're a restaurant; you have paying customers, leave the "don't care" mentality at Phi Delt.

Recommended Dish: Green Curry Chicken, $11.50; Chicken Satay, $5.50

Market Table

I love Allechante. For those of you who don't know, Allechante is an artisan bakery in Norwich, VT. One day, someone in Allechante's marketing department realized that Dartmouth students are willing to pay any amount of money to think that they are cultured, so the artisans opened in Hanover and called it Market Table (I don't really get the name either).

Walking into Market Table, you see a spitting image of the Norwich bakery: a large display holding side dishes and the same list of sandwiches. The best part: **everything is just as delicious**. The fresh, local ingredients that made Allechante famous are mirrored in the new location – I recommend you try everything at least once. The other half of Market Table is a legitimate "sit-down" restaurant. The **ambience reminds me of something I would find in a big city** (the kitchen is open, so you can watch the chefs working), and the food is great if you are looking for a meal. Dishes include slow-cooked pork shoulder and a delicious miso glazed cod. Because they just opened, I let this slide, but Market Table will need to improve its service before it gets a Michelin star.

Recommended Dish: Misty Knoll Turkey Sandwich; Miso Glazed Cod

Molly's

When you try to do too much in college, you end up falling short (see pg. 75). Molly's should take this lesson to heart. Molly's is a **cheap bastardization of an Applebee's that has been decorated by the Dartmouth admissions office**. While I have always thought about the number of things I would steal from Molly's if I had the chance, its decorations don't make up for it's awful food. I have yet to find a dish that I have enjoyed.

The appetizers are too heavy on the sauce; the pizzas have one ingredient that overwhelms the whole dish; even the "world famous" mac-and-cheese is too heavy to enjoy. These dishes are neither experimental nor technically difficult, so I can't, for the life of me, understand why the chefs at Molly's can't properly cook a burger medium-rare yet. However, even I have to admit that **when a warm loaf of Molly's bread is placed in front of me alongside their honey-butter, I have to dig in**.

And maybe once you're legal, try one of the $2.00 Margaritas. Even though they're not the strongest drink ever made, they are cheap enough to make for a fun pre-meetings pre-game that won't hurt your wallet. Molly's, like most Dartmouth students, is just trying too hard.

Recommended Dish: *Molly's bread and honey-butter, complimentary; Margarita, $2.00*

Morano Gelato

I like to consider myself an ice cream aficionado. My palate is advanced enough to tell the difference between gelato, sorbet, and ice cream. I've been to the best places in New York: Grom, Chinatown Ice Cream Factory, L'Arte del Gelato. So when I impart this advice, take it seriously. Morano Gelato is **one of the best gelaterias in all of North America** – that is not an exaggeration.

Every gelato is creamy, smooth, and flavorful. The owner worked under a Sicilian gelato chef in Italy, and she uses only the highest quality ingredients and the most advanced gelato-making technology. Now that Morano has moved out of the basement of Rosie Jekes, what more could you want after a long day on the Green. If Morano has an IPO, I would get in on that early. Blue Horseshoe loves Morano Gelato.

Recommended Dish: *Small cup of any flavor, $3.00*

Murphy's on the Green

My relationship with Murphy's has had its ups and downs. Four years ago Murphy's was a b-side Molly's. The food was unmemorable and the atmosphere was stuffy. Sometime around Sophomore Summer, someone finally stood up and said, "We suck. Maybe we should do something about it." Two years later, we have one of my favorite restaurants in Hanover.

Many of the dinner dishes at Murphy's are great. They unfortunately got rid of their signature beef medallions (pieces of perfectly cooked steak), but luckily, the chef kept the Murph Burger for hoards of hungry college students to enjoy. Moreover, Murphy's has **some of the best appetizers I have ever had in my life**. The Buffalo wings are delicious: crispy-on-the-outside, tender-on-the-inside, the right amount of sauce, and a perfect balance between spice and vinegar. Even more delicious are the nachos. Covered in cheese, pinto beans, pickled jalapeños, and chili - perfect for sharing.

Finally, Murphy's has an extensive bar with a great selection of local beers both on tap and in the bottle. Murphy's has transformed itself into the best gastro-pub from here to Boston; use that information wisely over your four years.

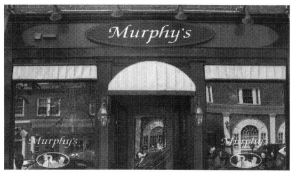

Recommended Dish: Nachos, $10.00; 24 Buffalo Wings, $16.00; Murph Burger, $13.00

The Orient

Would a college town be complete without grim Chinese food? Obviously not, and that's why the Orient exists. Let's just be honest, the Orient is the abandoned-bastard-child of a Chinatown dim sum and a Panda Express. For the adventurous types, the Orient boasts a variety of authentic Chinese dishes like rooster feet, bean curd, and multiple preparations of prawns; for everyone else there is General Tso's, Mongolian beef, and sesame chicken.

The **food is exactly what you expect: average quality, large**

portions, and heavy. The authors recommend going live with a group of friends because the first thing you will notice upon entering is that no one is ever in the Orient. Every other restaurant will have its slew of townies, but the Orient is perpetually empty – you honestly could do whatever you want in the back room, and no one would know.

Once you sit down, order one dish for every person and eat everything family style with a surprisingly alcoholic Scorpion Bowl to wash it down. Blame it on globalization, but grim Chinese food has become as much of a college staple as pizza, so indulge.

Recommended Dish: Peking Duck $13.95, General Tso's Chicken, $11.95

Ramunto's

Growing up, I had this idea of college that consisted of sustaining myself on pizza, beer, and Top Ramen. While I am glad to say that never came to fruition, I do have to mention Hanover's pizzeria, Ramunto's Brick and Brew. Given the plethora of underwhelming eateries in the area, you would expect Ramunto's to be a letdown, but it isn't; I'd even say it's actually pretty good.

First, apologies to the readers from Chicago, but the pizza is thin-crust, not deep-dish (everyone knows that deep-dish sucks anyway). Ramunto's does a great job kicking out pizzas extremely efficiently. Are the pizza's perfect every time? No. Could the sauce be fresher? Sure. Could the pizza be topped with fresh basil kept in the window seal? I guess. But **Ramunto's gets the job done, and when I am in the mood for pizza, I will go to Ramunto's** over any other restaurant in the area. You can order a re-heated slice from one the dozen pre-made pizzas or you can order a pie and a half-dozen garlic or cinnamon knots (Ramunto's take on breadsticks) with your friends. Fortunately, their **specialty pizzas are delicious** (one of the best BBQ Chicken Pizza I've ever had), and, of course, Ramunto's also offers a variety of very good beers on tap. Better yet, delivery usually takes under an hour, so get over your desire to be "unique" at Dartmouth and just do the whole pizza and beer thing.

Recommended Dish: Large BBQ Chicken Pizza, $19.99

Salt Hill Pub

Salt Hill Pub recently opened a new location in downtown Hanover; but to call Salt Hill a pub is a little overzealous. The decorations are a little too contrived (a Guinness soccer jersey, really?), the seating is a little too restaurant-like, and the whole place is a little too clean to call it a pub. Salt Hill might be the only restaurant in the area where **you get exactly what you expect**.

The food is average, some dishes are pretty good, but nothing is great. The burgers might come a little overcooked, the chicken might be too dry for your liking, but never to such a degree where you would never come back. Living in the bustling metropolis that is Hanover, you need to realize that you can't ask for much.

The most important thing to understand is that all of **the American dishes are great, and all of the Irish ones are terrible**. You can eat all the typical pub fare you want (buffalo wings, onion rings, burgers, etc.) and there are plenty of beers on tap at a price that is a marginally cheaper than Murphy's. Some people have argued that the pulled pork nachos are even better than Murphy's chili nachos, but those people are wrong. Salt Hill isn't overly ambitious in what it's trying to get done, and I appreciate that.

Recommended Dish: *Judy's Hand Battered Green Pepper Rings, $5.29, The Jake Burger (Bacon, Cheddar, and a fried egg), $8.29*

Umpelby's

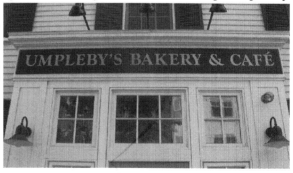

Capitalism has slowly found its way into Hanover. The poor quality of some restaurants can often be explained by the lack of competition in the area – it doesn't have to be perfect if there is no where else to go, AMIRIGHT?!?! Luckily, Umpleby's Bakery and Café has come into the market as the largest (only) competitor with the Dirt Cowboy. Umpleby's has a substantially larger seating area than Dirt, has much better lighting, and doesn't have an incessant, cacophonous background noise. Sounds like a perfect place to do work right? Too bad it is unreasonably far away (relatively – it's only an extra two blocks). The location of the Dirt Cowboy is unbeatable, and in all honesty the Cowboy has the edge in coffee, but Umpleby's provides a legitimate alternative if need be. In terms of food, the specials change every day, and the **chicken chili is delicious**. Umpleby's has two displays, one of savory pies and one of colorful sweets, which are all actually pretty good. Some of the pies are in desperate need of some sort of sauce to cut the dryness, but **the sandwiches, especially the bread, are definitely worth a try**.

Recommend Dish: Curried chicken pie $4.50; Chicken Chili $3.50

Yama

The sheer number of ethnic restaurants in Hanover doesn't make sense, but Yama somehow figured out how to make itself more popular than any other. **Yama is always packed**. The owners have a unique way of se'ating you: you walk into an absurdly small waiting area, write your name and party size down on a piece of paper, and just wait. You can try to ask how long they think it will be, but it's likely to be 15 minutes, no matter how many people are in front of you.

Yama is a Korean restaurant at heart, but to fill the niche they also offer a variety of sushi. Realize that you won't be getting the finest cuts of ootoro, but if you know what ootoro is, you probably realized that as soon as you walked through the door. The **Korean dishes, however, are very good**. When you sit down at Yama, you are given a half-dozen Korean appetizers (banchan) that are fun to fumble with while attempting to show off your chopstick skills.

The kopdol bibimbab (specifying kopdol is necessary because the food is served in an extremely hot stone bowl that continues to cook the rice into a nice crisp) is the best item on the menu. Rice, steamed vegetables, meat, and a fried egg, all covered in spicy sauce, the bibimbab kopdol is simple yet delicious. Items like the bulgoki and kalbi are pretty good. Finally, Yama of course serves sake bombs. But, it's extremely uncomfortable when the whole restaurant stops eating and looks at you after you sake bomb; but, hey, facetime is cool.

Recommended dish: Kopdol bibimbab, $9.95, Beef Mandu soup, $3.95

*Zin's Winebistro: please never go here.

Upper Valley Dining

Experts Only

This section is only for the most elite Upper Valley diners. Most of these restaurants will never be experienced by your peers, but with all that the Upper Valley has to offer, you would be making a huge mistake by not going to at least a few of these. Obviously, a car is necessary to enjoy some of these great attractions:

* - A very good restaurant in its category
** - Excellent cooking and worth a detour
*** - Exceptional cuisine and worth the journey

Allechante** (Norwich, Vermont)
The quaint artisan bakery.
Situated across the Connecticut River, Allechante offers an amazing selection of sandwiches and fresh, local side dishes (chicken fingers, pulled pork, salads, etc). In the spring and summer, make the walk from Hanover to Allechante and enjoy one of their delicious sandwiches or unbelievable desserts made daily.

Big Fatty's (Hartford, Vermont)
The local barbeque joint.
If you want pounds of pulled pork, venture over to Big Fatty's. For the hard guys who are trying to make a name for themselves, try and get your name on the wall by finishing the Big Fatty's challenge.

Carpenter and Main*** (Norwich, Vermont)
The Best Food Around.
Offering an awe-inspiring selection of well-prepared dishes that can be best described as French fusion, Carpenter and Main is where you should take your parents every time they come to visit. The escargot, rabbit three ways, and crispy duck confit are all cooked to perfection and could be presented in the best New York City restaurants.

Cuttings Northside Café (Hanover, New Hampshire)
The inside joke.
Located North of campus on Route 10, Cuttings has become an inside joke in the Dartmouth community. The gossip website Bored@Baker glorifies their "piping-hot calzones" and arcade-quality pizza.

Farmer's Diner* (Quechee, Vermont)
The Hidden Diner.
Farmer's Diner is a few steps away from the Quechee Gorge in Vermont. An actual dining car with a restaurant attached, Farmer's Diner offers a variety of breakfast and lunch foods. While the service is sometimes questionable, their breakfast foods are cooked extremely well.

Fire Stone's (Quechee, Vermont)
The village pizza.
This one is really rogue. Most people will never go to Fire Stone's, but if you ever find yourself in Quechee and in need of affordable food, Fire Stone's may be your place. Located in a very quintessential New England storefront village, Fire Stone's offers a variety of flatbreads, pizzas, and pastas.

Fort Lou's (Lebanon, New Hampshire)
The Proletariat's Lou's.
Fort Lou's is a 24-hour breakfast restaurant located in a truck-stop right off of I-89. Usually reserved for the 4 a.m. adventure, Fort Lou's offers the same menu of items as Lou's, but Fort Lou's cooks them much worse.

Jesse's (Hanover, New Hampshire)
The sign on the road.
You'll see the sign for Jesse's as you drive into Hanover, it's impossible to miss. Known for their steak and lobster, Jesse's is outstanding in its mediocrity.

Lui Lui's (West Lebanon, New Hampshire)
The Italian Molly.
Molly's decided to put on some designer clothing and create a restaurant of equivalent poor quality, but with an Italian accent.

Margarita's (Hanover, New Hampshire)
The Mexican Molly.
Translate above description into Spanish.

Norwich Inn (Norwich, Vermont)
The Hanover Inn with beer.
Like many inns in the area, the Norwich Inn has a restaurant attached to its hotel. The food is actually decent and the ambience is great (think

fireplace, lots of couches and tables, small bar with the stereotypical New England bartender). They have a cellar room that can be rented out for large groups, and even make their own beer – although the beer isn't that great.

Osteria Pane e Salute** (Woodstock, Vermont)
The high-brow Italian spot.
If you knew about this place before you read this book, I will be extremely impressed. The boutique restaurant is very small, but specializes in authentic, delicious Italian cooking. They have an award-winning wine bar, and their chefs often travel around the country on book-tours. If you are trying to sound like a foodie, head here.

Peyton Place** (Orford, New Hampshire)
The cutest place around.
Now this place could make even the hardest guy's heart melt, it's super quaint (they have hundreds of woven baskets hanging from the ceiling) and unbelievably New England. Focusing on only the freshest ingredients, the menu is written on a chalk board every night. If you are trying to be romantic take your girlfriend here for Valentine's day and reap the benefits.

The Red Rooster-Woodstock Inn* (Woodstock, Vermont)
The Hanover Inn on steroids.
Walking in may be daunting (stick to the left, the restaurant is there I promise), but the restaurant in the Woodstock Inn is definitely worth a peak. The food is good, the decorations are beautiful, and the wide open space with plenty of natural light makes it seem like the kind of restaurant you would eat brunch in on the Upper East Side. The food is reasonably priced, but be careful, the drinks are expensive.

Seven Barrel Brewery (West Lebanon, New Hampshire)
The poor attempt.
West Lebanon is proof that not everyone can be an urban planner. Located on the strip is an actual brewery that makes beer that is so watery that makes Keystone taste like an Imperial IPA. The food is bad, the drinks aren't great, but I appreciate the effort.

Simon Pearce*** (Quechee, Vermont)
The definition of New England.
Dear Simon Pearce, you are what restaurants should strive to be, Love, GREEN. The famous glass blowing shop has one of the most beautiful restaurants in existence. They offer seasonal cuisine with a strong local focus (amazing fish specials) and are located on top of a small waterfall, which makes the views unbeatable. Unbelieavbly romantic, dinner or brunch at Simon Pearce will make you realize why you want to be in New England.

Stella's* (Lyme, New Hampshire)
The mid-level Italian spot.
The drive is a little longer than you expect, but the Italian-American food served at Stella's is slightly better than expectation. With a variety of wines, local cheeses, and delicious appetizers, Stella's is a good place to go with the family.

Three Tomatoes (Lebanon, New Hampshire)
The beginner's Italian spot.
You've decided to eat somewhere outside of Hanover, congratulations! Three Tomatoes is your baby step. Located on the Green in Lebanon (bet you didn't know they had one, too), Three Tomatoes offers average Italian-American fare. The pastas might not be al dente, but the brick-oven pizzas are pretty good and cheap.

Tip Top Café (White River Junction, Vermont)
The hip new shop.
Tip top café is located in a new, extremely modern office building in White River Junction. If you can get past all of the decorations, Tip Top has some great food (try the fries). When the weather gets nice, you can sit on their terrace and enjoy a great dinner.

Weathervane (West Lebanon, New Hampshire)
The seafood shack.
From the outside it looks like a wood shack, on the inside it looks like Long John Silver's. But Weathervane offers a comical amount of deep fried seafood and unbelievably cheap lobster. You won't get sick eating there, but you won't feel great afterwards, either.

VIII

Drinking

"Lines are long, but I've seen longer..."

George Jung

Stinson's Village Store
Jack: The Man, The Myth, The Enabler

In ancient times, scientists believed that the universe revolved around the Earth. More specifically, they believed that it revolved around Jerusalem. How foolish of them. **Today, scientists know that the universe revolves around Stinson's Village Store.**

Stinson's, located on Allen Street (off Main Street) is the fountain from which Dartmouth's alcohol pours. There's a rumor going around that 1% of all Keystone Light sold in the world is sold at Stinson's. Jury's still out on whether or not the rumor's true, but the fact that it's still around has to mean that it's close enough to the truth. Social chairs drive into the alley behind the store every night and make off with hundreds upon hundreds of cases.

Who is Jack Stinson, you may ask? Don't ask that question aloud, since it will reveal idiocy. **Jack Stinson is a man that every Dartmouth student should meet.** The College is actually considering adding something about Jack Stinson to the graduation requirements. Instead of being able to pass the swim test, you'll have to pass the Stinson's Story test, in which you will be asked for your best Jack Stinson story and must provide it. If you're able to convincingly tell a rendition of the time when Jack invited you over to his house and you babysat his kids while he went to a monster truck rally, then you'll get a bid at any house you want and will give the valedictory address at Commencement.

Even if you're too young to buy beer (Stinson's I.D.s!), you can still go to Stinson's for all your other fixations: candy, energy drinks, cigarettes, dip, snus, gum, whatever. Go there frequently. Chat up Jack and all the nice ladies there about anything. You'll start getting **free shit at Stinson's, the Dartmouth equivalent of an Amex Black Card.**

Overheards

{ Because **Alumni** say the darn'dest things! }

{ BITTER ALUM (POST LOSS): "WE PLAYED A DIFFERENT KIND OF PONG WHEN I WAS HERE... NONE OF THIS 'LOB' SHIT!" }

(INSERT ANY FRATERNITY OR DDS ITEM) "LOOKS THE SAME, SMELLS THE SAME, TASTES THE SAME..."

"HOW YOUNG IS TOO YOUNG?"

SENIOR ALUM (POST BOOT): "TASTES LIKE 1957!"

ALUM #1: "HAVE YOU DONE THE ALUMNI DARTMOUTH SEVEN YET?"
ALUM #2: "NO... WHAT ARE THOSE?"
ALUM #1: "WELL, HOW DO YOU FEEL ABOUT IMPROVISATION..."

ALUM #1: "GO DARTMOUTH FOOTBALL!"
ALUM #2: "ARE YOU SENILE?"

DRINKING

Pong

This is like Beirut, right?

Oh pong, where to begin? Retaining its status as the ubiquitous mode of alcohol consumption across Dartmouth's campus for over a half century, this game has become interwoven into the social fabric of Hanover itself. If you haven't heard of pong before you get to Dartmouth, chances are you will be talking about it within fifteen minutes of stepping off the Dartmouth Coach.

Invented at Dartmouth in the early 50's, legend has it that two fraternity brothers were playing ping pong while drinking beer (a stand-up idea on its own) when one put his cup down on the table, and the other hit the ball in. Like the moment when the apple hit Newton on the head, a beautiful idea was born: modern competitive drinking games. Due to the flexible nature of the game and the Ivy-League intellectual restlessness present in the Dartmouth student body, countless variations of pong have emerged, so we will do our best to cover the most popular versions. The rules below explain the main version of Hanover's beloved past-time.

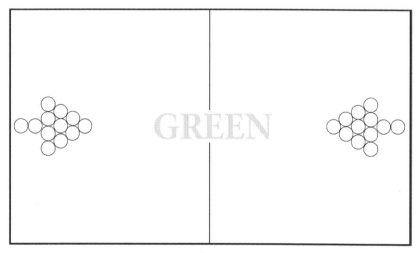

Required Materials
- Four people, two per team
- Cups: 12 oz. clear plastic cups. Seven for shrub, eleven for single-stem tree, twelve for double-stem tree, or 9 for death/line
- Paddles: four sandpaper ping-pong paddles with the handle broken off

- Beer: four for shrub, six for single-stem tree, seven for do tree, or five for death/line
- Table: A 9'x5' or 10'x5' piece of wood elevated to about wai. (usually on two trash cans)
- Median: This demarcates the two sides of the table and can be anything ranging from a golf club, ski, shoe lace, or drawn-in line.
- Set-up: Reference the diagrams shown to decide which form of the game you would like to play and set up the cups accordingly.

Game Play

1. The object of pong is to clear the table of an opponent's cups by hitting them or sinking them.
2. The game begins with some high school Beirut in order to decide which team serves first. It is sudden death, so if the first team to shoot sinks, the opposing team must sink in order for the rally to continue. The losing team serves first.
3. The Serve: every rally begins with a serve from the team that lost the preceding point. The serve must be a "lay-up" i.e. a high lob to the opponent diagonally across from the server. More experienced players learn to put spin on their serve in order to make it more difficult for the opponent to hit the cups off his/her serve.
    a. If a cup is hit or sunk on a serve by the server, he/she must drink the equivalent amount of his/her formation. The receiving team chooses which cup they would like the other team to drink.
    b. You cannot lose on a serve. If a player hits an opponent's formation on a serve when he/she only has one half cup left, then the serving resumes as if it never happened.
    c. Aces: This occurs when a serve nicks the side of the table and does not touch the receiving players paddle. Some fraternities deem this event a half cup penalty for the receiving team, some do not count it at all, and others have more dubious rules for this occasion (GDX... gross).
4. The Rally: during game play, all hits must be lobbed shots. "Low" can be called at any time in the game by either team if a shot is not a lob. It is common courtesy to call your own shots and sportsmanship plays a large role here. Partners in this game alternate every shot.
    a. Hits – If a cup is "hit" during play and not subsequently saved, the team whose cups were hit must drink half of said cup. Again, for those non-math majors, two hits and a cup is then removed from the game. When the ball has bounced

twice on the table or has hit the floor, the point is dead and a hit has occurred.

b. Saves – If a cup is hit, the receiving team has an opportunity to "save" the point. This happens when the ball takes a maximum of one bounce on the table and is subsequently hit back on the other half of the table by the receiving team. The "low" rule does not apply to saves, and the return of a saved shot must only be higher than the save itself. Regular "low" rules resume after the save return.

    i. Team-Saves – This rule is used by over half of the fraternities on campus. This rule of saving says that when a cup is hit, either player on the receiving team can return the ball for a save.

    ii. Individual-Saves – Commonly referred to as "No Team-Saves," this rule states that only the person who is about to hit the next shot may save the ball.

    iii. Slam-Saves – Played by most houses on campus, this event occurs when a ball takes a convenient bounce after a hit and is subsequently slammed across to the other side of the table. This shot has advantages over a regular save in that it is virtually un-returnable and if it hits the opposing team's cups, it is very difficult to save.

    iv. Throw-Saves – If on a hit, a ball bounces out of reach for the person trying to save, he/she may throw their paddle in order to force the ball over the halfway line. Careful though, this method of saving is certainly an art form and can get very messy before it is eventually mastered.

    v. Body-Saves – Played by a smaller number of houses on campus, this method of saving lends itself to the more skilled pong players. If a shot or save seems un-returnable due to whatever circumstance, the player about to hit may use his/her body (arms/hands not included) to buoy the ball into a more convenient space to hit the ball with his/her paddle. Moves include the chest-bump, the header, and the coveted kick-save. The ball may only bounce once on the table, hit a player's body, and then be returned for a good save. The order cannot go body-table-save.

    vi. Kick-Saves – Probably the hardest thing to accomplish

in pong, this method of saving occurs when a player kicks a seemingly impossible to reach ball out of the air and subsequently returns the ball to the opposing players half. If team-saves are not in place, a player attempting a kick save who is not up to hit may only try to kick the ball over to their teammate.
      vii. Blow Saves – Are you kidding? Hey Theta Delt!
   c. Sinks – A sink occurs when the ball lands in a cup. The cup is subsequently drunk and discarded by the receiving team. That's it.
5. The Playmaker (only played at AD and Theta Delt): This rule, implemented by two frat brothers inadvertently playing pong on an Indian burial ground, states that if the middle cup in the formation is sunk on the first shot (saves not included) of a player's game, the receiving team must drink the back four cups in the formation. Be wary, though, the playmaker is said to be cursed…
6. End: a game is finished when one team's cups have been completely removed from the table.
7. Etiquette: Pong is a gentlemen's game, and a certain standard of etiquette is expected to be displayed in the basement by each and every player.
   a. Elaborate celebrations are haughty, ostentatious, and usually pretty stupid looking. Save it for the sororities (looking at you freshmen and tennis players).
   b. Call your own shots low. It is your responsibility to do this, although the other team might help you out with your decision if a shot is questionable, usually via questioning looks and passive aggressive remarks.
   c. Don't slam-save on a pong date (see pg. 88), asshole.
   d. Don't spin serve on a pong date, douchebag.
   e. Sportsmanship should be displayed at all times. If you lose a game you think you shouldn't have lost, don't be condescending and self-righteous, shake the hands of those fortunate freshmen and get on with your life (which can include bumping those lucky-ass freshmen and regaining your pride).

Alternate Formations

There are several different versions of pong played at Dartmouth, with some versions unique to individual fraternities. Sorry if we did not document 'your' version. Stick to these and you should be just fine.

Single-Stem Shrub

Played at: AXA, BG, Tri-Kap, Psi U, SAE, Zete, EKT, KDE, SD

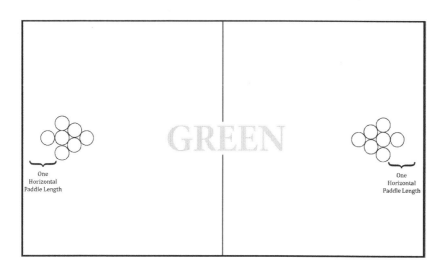

Single-Stem Tree

Played at: Phi Delt, XH, Beta, GDX

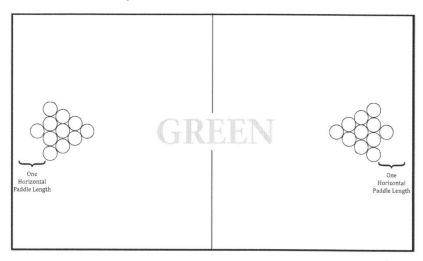

<u>Line / Death</u>

Played at: Sig Ep, Sig Nu

<u>Double-Stem Tree</u>

Played at: AD, TDX

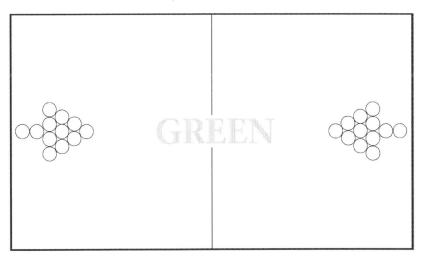

Harbor

'Cause you have nothing better to do...

One of the more popular, yet mildly competitive, social games on campus, Harbor is said to have originated in the Tower Room bathroom in the spring of 1994. Looking to procrastinate from their arduous finals grind, two students were playing battle-shits after a twenty-one cup coffee binge, when a genius idea plopped into their heads: turn this classic finals past-time into an explosively popular drinking game. From this, Harbor bore its head.

Set Up

- Follow the above diagram in order to set up the game correctly. For those non-math majors, the formations (boats) are made up of six, five, four, three, two, then one (the mine) cups. That's twenty-one cups and ~fourteen beers per team.
- The teams are made up of two players, with each team defending one of the four corner-ship formations, and each player with his/her own paddle.
- Only one ball necessary
- Place medians as diagram shows.

Game Play

1. The game begins with a random team starting with the ball and serving it up to any of the other three teams on the table. The serve should be a lay-up and although not a rule, it is extremely bad etiquette to hit back at the serving teams cup's after being laid-up.
2. Regular rules of pong apply for hits, sinks, and saves. The cups should be removed from outside in, though. So if the cup on the left end of the six-boat is sunk, remove the right end full. If one of the inner-boat cups is 'sunk', remove that cup and move the rest of the cups down so that there are no gaps in the boat.
3. Also, the rule of "low" concerning shots is generally ignored, unless the shot is a blatant slam not on a save.
4. Teamwork is crucial in harbor, especially communication. There is no standard switch of turns like regular pong, so deciding which teammate is hitting the ball in your quadrant requires regular communication and an understanding of your partner's pong ability, footwork, and positioning.
5. Sinkability: once a boat is battered down to 2.5 cups or less, this specific boat becomes "sinkable". If a cup in this boat is sunk at any point in the game, the team defending that cup must drink the whole boat.
6. The Mine: This is the lone cup in the formation, placed at the back corner between the four, five, and six cup boats. If an opposing team hits or sinks this cup, the offender must run over to the cup, drink the appropriate amount (half for a hit, full for a sink), if emptied, fill the cup back up, and return. Different tactics can be employed by the opposing fleets in this situation. One strategy employable by the other three teams is to yell "Attack!" and send a barrage of hits towards the team with only one player to defend the ships. Reverse psychology can also be employed by the depleted team and their allies (see Rule 8) by yelling "No Mine!" which implies the team whose mine is being drunk can now be hit at without fear of hitting the dreaded single cup.
7. Saving: In order for a save to be considered good, it must leave the quadrant of the defending team. Absolutely no throw saves. If your paddle leaves your hand at any point during the motion of a save, you must drink the cup it hit whether or not the save ended up being good and suffer the verbal abuse inevitably coming your way.
8. Alliances: An alliance can be formed secretly between any two teams at any time. But beware, these partnerships are by no means binding and betrayals are common.

9. Electricity: This rule states that every cup that is touched by the ball during a hit before the ball lies dead must be considered "hit" and drunk accordingly.
10. Elimination: Whenever a team's boats have been fully eliminated bar the mine, they are expelled from the game. Upon this shameful and emotional event, the other teams remaining add insult to injury by chanting, "Na, na, na, na; na, na, na, na; hey, hey, hey; goodbye!" The remaining teams repeat this ceremonial song twice while slamming their paddles on the table in order to keep the beat and alert everyone else around of the eliminated team's shameful and embarrassing situation.
11. End-Game: After two of the four teams have been eliminated from the battle, the game is consolidated down to two quadrants i.e. one table. Each team takes its remaining cups and forms a formation as close to shrub or tree as possible. A game of regular pong ensues following the rules of the specific house the game was played in. Simply put, the team to hit the last half wins! They can subsequently rejoice in probably the most meaningless victory in anything they have ever done, which is usually accomplished by playing another game.

PongFlip

A hybrid of two favorites

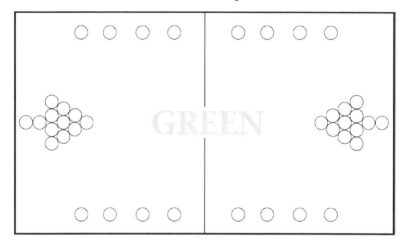

Played on a standard pong table, PongFlip can accommodate any even number of players - making it an excellent game for a group of people at a party looking to get lubricated together. The game consists of two teams, each with a tree or shrub formation. A normal game of pong commences with two people on each end of the table. The rest the players are lined up along the table, each with a 1/4 filled cup of beer in front of them. If a cup is sunk, the flip cup game begins at the end of the table where the cup was sunk. The team whose cup is sunk acts as the defending team, and if this team wins the flipcup game, they successfully defend their cup and the sunken cup remains in the game. If the offensive team wins the flipcup game, then the sunken cup is removed from the table. Hits that result in missed saves are indefensible and the defending team drinks half of a cup.

- To incentivize longer points, if a player ends the point by hitting the ball off the table, he/she switches positions with a flipcup teammate.

- A pong player also subs out if the other team hits or sinks a cup after his/her shot.

- The four pong players in a particular point where a cup is sunk join the end of the flipcup lines, resulting in an all-inclusive flipcup game to decide the fate of a sunk cup.

Social

So Fun!

There are no nuances behind the title of this game. This form of pong is often played with a mix of guys and girls and is the least competitive of the pong variations explained in this book. It is commonly played by couples before sorority and Chi Gam formals, large groups trying to collectively pre-game a sporting event, and AD's at 4:30 a.m. on a Monday.

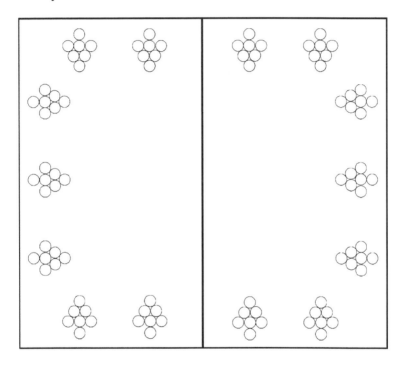

Setup
- Follow the above diagram in order to set up correctly. Social is not confined to a certain amount of players or formations, though; any number of people can play, so add additional pong tables as necessary in order to accommodate your group.
- There are no teams in this game, and each player plays with his/her own shrub or tree of beer, depending on how long everyone wants to play or how rowdy they plan on getting.
- Any number of balls can be used in order to play Social, but as the great Craven Laycock once said, "The more the better..."

Game Play

1. Social is a simple game with simple rules. Hits are a half cup, sinks are a full cup out, just like regular pong.
2. The game is a free-for-all. The object is to be the last man standing, so anyone's cups are game to aim at.
3. If a ball is hit long or off the table, slams are usually in effect. This happens when the ball takes one bounce after being hit long and is subsequently hit at another Social player. If a player is hit cleanly with a slam, he/she must drink a half cup, unless they only have one half cup left; you cannot lose on a slam.
4. When serving, a simple lay up to someone close to you will do.
5. Low calls happen very rarely, as this rule is usually ignored unless it is blatant.
6. Saves must leave the general area of the players cups in order to count
7. Distractions to other players via flirtation or intimidation are highly encouraged but please exclude tactics such as indecent exposure, tickling, and touching of the hair or face.

IX

Greek Life

"Fat, drunk, and stupid is no way to go through life, son [daughter]."

Dean Wormer, *Animal House*

The Greek System
An Overview of Overviews

    The Greek system at Dartmouth is bigger than Miley Cyrus; it's bigger than my body; it's well, bigger than... a lot of big things. More than Homecoming, more than the football team, more than any class. It is the air we breathe. It's where many of us live, where most of us socialize casually, and where almost all of us drink.
    The Greek system formally started at Dartmouth in May of 1842 with the forming of the first national fraternity chapter on campus, Psi Upsilon. Psi U was followed shortly by the first local fraternity, Kappa Kappa Kappa, in July of that same year. Following this, many fraternities were started, with seemingly more every year.
    Over time, some rose and some fell, and **Dartmouth eventually settled on its current level, around 15.** In the 1950's and 60's, many fraternities split off from their nationals over various disagreements. For example, many nationals didn't allow black or Jewish members and the progressive Dartmouth frats weren't about to abide by that. Then, almost immediately after coeducation hit Dartmouth in 1972, five local fraternities decided to become co-ed, which forms the root of today's co-ed environment. In 1977, Sigma Kappa (now Sigma Delta), the College's first sorority was formed. The **sorority presence on campus has been steadily increasing since then.**
    In 1999, College President James Wright announced the Student Life Initiative, which was the largest shift in the Greek system since coeducation. His plan was summarized in his oft-quoted line, "... to end the Greek system as we know it." We saw increased college oversight of

parties, keg regulation, and a set of strictly enforced minimum standards that gave the entire Greek system a series of long-overdue physical renovations that made the houses safe and livable environments as opposed the dilapidated, shitty brick shacks that they had been.

Some people will tell you Dartmouth's Greek system revolves around drinking. That's definitely true. Others will tell you it's about brother/sisterhood and forming lifelong connections. That's got some truth to it, too. Some people see it as just a social space. That's fine, too.

Your first encounter with the Greek system will come during Orientation, in all likelihood. You'll play pong with one of your trip leaders at a quieter Greek house, or you'll go to a party at some louder Greek house.

Things you should know before you even approach the Greek scene:
1. Anybody can go in anywhere
2. The beer (Keystone Light) is $Free.99
3. Don't ask for anything else, because the beer is all you'll get
4. Only brothers/sisters behind the bar
5. Dudes pee in the basement; ladies pee on the second floor
6. It's acceptable to ask for line at any table; it is not acceptable to complain about the answer you get

Your first time in a loud frat will probably be a flurry of different thoughts and feelings. Just drink up and **have a good time**. After a little while, you'll form a relationship with the Greek system. You like playing early p at this house, and the dance parties at that house are always the sickest. The dudes are kinda dicks in this other house. **You always feel small in GDX.**

Your sophomore fall, 60% of you will rush. I recommend it. Rush for girls is terrible, but pledge term is non-existent. Rush for guys is minimal and painless, and then pledge term varies from hectic to fun to just f*cking brutal. You'll get through it.

After that, you'll be a brother/sister, and what you do after that is up to you. Wanna hang out at your house all the time, play Harbor every night and try to be Sophomore Summer president? Cool, dude. Good luck. Wanna stay a social butterfly, hanging out lots of different places and probably not live in your Greek house? Lots of people do that, too. **What you do after that is up to you.** Either way, don't be surprised when you transition from a high school senior who never thought of being in a Greek house to a college sophomore, balls deep in the system and loving every second of it.

Greek Philanthropy

Giving back

Contrary to what you may think, **Greek life at Dartmouth is not all about pong, hooking up, and rocking sweet gear**. Don't get me wrong, all that stuff is important, but another key aspect of Greek life is community service (make sure to tell this part to your mom). The IFC and PanHell, as well as individual fraternities and sororities **play a large role in Dartmouth's outreach efforts to the local community.** Through financial contributions, volunteer efforts, and fundraising drives, the Dartmouth Greek community is an active participant in the campaign to improve the lives of others.

Listing every service event that every house does is impossible, but several significant efforts stand out. Over the summer, Dartmouth fraternities and sororities are heavily involved in the Prouty, a bike rice to raise money for cancer research. With nearly every house participating in some form, the Greek community helped raise over $20,000 this past year. Recently, the IFC was heavily involved in Project Right Choice, a Dartmouth-led group that seeks to raise awareness for important issues and works to address them. In the past two years, the IFC helped Project Right Choice raise over $25,000 for wounded veterans and over $20,000 for clean drinking water in Africa. Every fall, the houses on Webster Ave. host a well-attended Halloween Trick or Treat event for local children. This past year, the event received significant attention in the local media. Other events include the Tri-Delt pancake breakfast for cancer research, the AD whiffle ball tournament for the HIV/AIDS awareness program, Grassroots Soccer, Psi U's annual participation in suicide prevention efforts, and the Tri-Kap Easter Egg Hunt for local children. Members of Greek houses are extremely involved in DREAM, a mentoring program for troubled Upper Valley youth, and coach local sports teams.

Dartmouth Greek houses are acutely aware of the potential they have to contribute positively to the world around them, and make a conscious effort to do so.

Dartmouth
Fraternities

"Grab a brew. Don't cost nothin'."

John "Bluto" Blutarsky, 1978

Understanding This Section

The content for almost every fraternity in this section was created by brothers in that particular house and moderately edited by the GREEN editors.

Each page contains a brief overview of the house to give a picture of what it is like from an 'objective' standpoint. Then there is a fan and hater section that is meant to give the reader an idea of what is said about these houses. It's important to remember that **almost** every profile was written by a brother from his respective house.

The houses are also graded for parties, athleticism, and academics. The editors of GREEN graded each house and based their decisions solely on objective factors, of course...

Keep in mind that the fraternities' brotherhoods and reputations change with time. The way GREEN portrays each fraternity is reflective of each fraternity's reputation, but is **by no means FACT**. Take what you read with one or two grains of salt and everyone should be just fine.

Rush Do's and Do Not's

From Two Former Rush Chairs

Do: Rush a fraternity - Whether you like it or not, Dartmouth's social scene is dominated by the Greek system. So embrace it and shop around, you never know where you might fit in and make some life-long friends and memories.

Don't: Talk shit about Keystone - No one cares how "good" the beer you and your high school friends snuck out of your parents stash was.

Do: Go out on Mondays - These nights tend to be generally more low key, but are also a great chance to play pong as a freshman and have substantive conversations with brothers.

Don't: Name drop - This means referencing other brothers you may know in the house when meeting a brother for the first time. They don't care that you played JV soccer at Roxbury Latin with the current Tech Chair.

Do: Hang out with brothers outside of the fraternity - Outside of Monday night (or off night) pong, the best settings to get to know the brothers in a specific house (and for them to get to know you) are outside the party scene. Any current or past fraternity member will agree that some of the best intra-fraternity male bonding happens outside the party scene.

Don't: Trash talk - Bashing other fraternities in order to get a bid to one of their social rivals displays a lack of tact, a lack of class, and a lack of anything better to talk about. Due to the small student population, chances are the brother with whom you are man-flirting has good friends in many other frats on campus. In addition, you may think you know enough to form an accurate opinion on each frat after reading the next section, which is perfectly reasonable, but you actually don't. The frats and their member make-up change gradually (hey, Sig Nu!), or suddenly (hey, Beta!), so give each one a chance before you form your biases.

Do: Shop around – Just because you like one frat because a movie happened to be based on it, or because your specific sport/club team has a high membership ratio does not mean it is the right frat for you. Give every house a chance before you make your final rush decision.

Don't: Get picked up – And if you do, **don't tell the police officer where you were drinking, you don't have to (see pg. 82).**

Alpha Delta
"AD"

The first thing you'll think when you enter AD is, "Jesus God Almighty, what is that smell?" The source of the smell is the gorf, an open sewer in the basement where brothers and guests can be seen peeing and booting freely.

Most of the brothers are athletes on the Rugby, Soccer, or Squash teams. Those not on teams make an effort to stay in varsity-athlete condition by smoking as much "tobacco" as possible, playing pong, and then smoking more. AD has one of the largest brotherhoods on campus and is a local fraternity, having broken off from its national in 1969 over numerous disagreements. While at times hard to believe, AD typically boasts the highest fraternity GPA on campus. The basement, in addition to featuring the gorf, gets repainted each term to update the obscene jokes and inside references that the brothers write on the walls. Highlights include: "Sodomize Intolerance" and **"Waldo: 1 Osama: 0"**.

A fan of the house would mention the ragers that AD regularly throws and the liberating feeling of peeing on the walls. If you head to a soccer game in the fall, you're likely to enjoy the humorous heckling of AD brothers; they have their own section reserved at field-level.

A hater would say that AD's consider themselves too cool for school, and that hater would probably be right.

AD's are most likely seen wearing some sweet team gear that got bequested down to them. You can tell that because the shirt has holes in it, smells, and has other dudes' names written in it.

Parties: A	Athletics: A-	Academics: A

Heard at the pregame:
"Shout"

Notable Parties:
White Party, Lawn Party

Drink of Choice:
Gorf Juice

Neighbors: Heorot

Alpha Chi Alpha
"Alpha Chi"

AXA's membership is drawn from across campus, except varsity athletics. Even the club soccer tradition has begun to wither. The tight brotherhood of AXA (voted best on campus two years running!!!) does however bring together the best musicians, scholars, intramural athletes, and do-nothings on campus.

Founded in the mists of the ancient past, AXA split from its national sometime in the mid-20th century. Renovations in the early 21st century added a beach volleyball court at the expense of the famed barn. The basement ceilings remain sadly low despite these renovations, but brothers play pong valiantly despite these impediments.

Alpha Chi's are best known for the red sirens they wear during pledge term: hate-like dome pieces that other bros occasionally attempt to steal as trophies. Do so at your own peril. AXA is also most known for its two iconic parties, the winter Beach Party featuring two tons of sand and live music, and the spring Pig Stick featuring two tons of food and live music.

Those who dislike AXA might complain that it's far off the beaten path, not trafficked by those looking to hook up, has a monotonously low key scene, and has really f*cking low ceilings.

Those who like AXA might gush that it is thankfully off the beaten path, not trafficked by those looking to hook up, reliably chill, and occasionally accepting of low hits.

| Parties: B- | Club Athletics: A | Academics: B+ |

Heard at the pregame:
"Love in This Club"

Notable Parties:
Pig Stick, Beach Party

Drink of Choice:
Varies by room

Neighbors: Sig Ep, EKT

Beta Alpha Omega
"Beta"

Officially known as Beta Alpha Omega, Beta was recently re-recognized by the College in 2008 after being de-recognized in the mid-1990's. The first few classes of brothers since then have comprised of athletes from just about every team around campus, including football, baseball, golf, track, lacrosse, rugby, and more, as well as debaters, entrepreneurs, social pioneers, and men of incredible academic standing. As a result of its recent re-recognition and its strong brotherly ties both past and present, Beta has an incredibly involved and generous alumni base.

Should you be lucky enough to stumble down Webster Ave. on a night when Beta is actually open, the sound of country music and southern accents will soon fill your ears. Though, once you get to know the brothers, you will learn that in fact only about four of them are actually from the South and the rest... well they like to dream.

A fan of the house will mention the pretty fun but infrequent parties Beta has each term. A female fan will tell you that the brothers are very respectful and warm towards women. Whether or not they have the most honorable intentions is irrelevant - at least they are gentlemanly in their pursuits.

A Beta Hater would complain about the exclusivity and lack of parties. You might hear things like, "They think they're so Southern-Fratty," and "Beta? I think I went in there once but I was too blacked out from the real parties to remember it. They have a nice TV, though."

Parties: B (arely)	Athletics: A-	Academics: A-

Heard at the pregame:
"Wagon Wheel"

Notable Parties:
Kappa Semi, Texas Two Step

Drink of Choice:
Southern Comfort

Neighbors: BG, Tri-Kap

Bones Gate
"BG"

This fraternity used to be known as Delta Tau Delta, but when they broke from their national in 1960 over a disagreement, they changed their name to Bones Gate, commonly shortened to "BG". That should give you a pretty good idea of the type of person who's a BG: the type of person who, if given the option, would name their fraternity "Bones Gate".

The brothers are hipsters, stoners, musicians, drinkers, Philosophy majors, or all of the above. They drink a good amount, despite the fact that they're generally dogshit at pong. To their credit, the reason why BG broke from their national was a disagreement over the national's racial policy; Delta Tau Delta didn't allow blacks or Jews, and the Dartmouth chapter wasn't OK with that. Progressivism!

A fan of the house would point to the fun parties that BG throws, and the diverse crowds that they attract. Girls also like 'hanging out' at BG when they're feeling guilty about 'chilling' at TDX too much and want to feel alternative.

A hater of BG would call the house pretentious and say that it's a bunch of boys from Westchester trying to rebel against their parents.

BG's are most likely seen wearing Ray-Bans (ironically!), a ubiquitous BG sweatshirt, a hyphy flat-brim, and have a Camel Light in between their lips and a James Joyce novel in their hands.

| Parties: B+ | Athletics: D | Academics: B |

Heard at the pregame:
"Cape Cod Kwassa Kwassa"

Notable Parties:
BG Te@, Cutter

Drink of Choice:
Te@

Neighbors: BETA, Sig Nu

Chi Gamma Epsilon
"Chi Gam"

Formerly known as Kappa Sigma, Chi Gam has been on the row for a long, long time and its reputation has recently undergone some serious revamping. For many years, it was the baseball house, but those athletes have since moved on to join their steaky brethren at GDX. Chi Gam also developed a "sketchy" reputation some time ago, for reasons not totally known, although some scholars contend that the recently removed dance floor stripper poles had something to do with it.

The house is primarily made up of lightweight rowers, ex-lightweight rowers and a very random smattering of nonners. Despite the lack of a dominant sports contingency or personality vibing out of the Gam, freshmen seem to flock to their intimate dance parties. Gammapalooza draws a solid crowd as one of the prime Green Key social events.

A fan of the House might say, "Chi Gam is a very relaxed place without any pressure or pretense in the basement. The guys are going after it and hanging out, but they're not trying too hard to fit a stereotype or mold. It's also always packed with freshmen, which is neat."

A hater of the House might say, "Oh my God. It's so sketchy there. Brothers always offer me drinks that are probably tainted. I mean I know it was an unopened can of Keystone, but like, you never know."

Brothers are most likely seen wearing a "Come As You Are" t-shirt or a lost Northface.

*Only Freshmen surveyed

| Parties: A* | Athletics: C+ | Academics: B+ |

Heard at the pregame:
"It Wasn't Me" -Shaggy

Notable Parties:
Gammapalooza

Drink of Choice:
Long Island Iced Tea

Neighbors: KDE, Phi Delt

Chi Heorot
"Heorot"

Its name is derived from the epic *Beowulf* in which Heorot, the feasting hall of the Danish warriors, is referred to as "the foremost of halls under heaven." Heorot's brotherhood consists primarily of athletes who excel on the water, snow, ice and track. Heorot was born after an ill-conceived attempt at turning the first floor into an indoor hockey rink destroyed the framing of the house. The incident resulted in the understandable divorce of Chi Phi from its national chapter and the creation of the local fraternity known simply as 'Heorot'.

Despite its roots in engineering disaster, the house's best features are its spacious first floor hall and cavernous basement. Pharaohs had the pyramids, Gladiators had the Coliseum, and pong players have the Heorot basement. For the player and spectator alike, the fraternity's basement is the premiere destination for all things pong. But where varsity pong players roam it's sink or be sunk, so bring your A-game.

Salty critics might say that Heorot is a one-trick pony when it comes to parties. They're probably right, but the house's hallmark party is always a banger. Also, the rays of enlightenment that emanate across the Dartmouth crest are traditionally unable to penetrate the hallowed halls of Heorot, which typically has the lowest house GPA on campus. Apparently good hockey IQ doesn't translate to the classroom.

Heorotians are most likely to be seen wearing tank tops emblazoned with their letters XH and perhaps a witty pong reference.

Parties: B+	Athletics: A	Academics: D+

Heard at the pregame:
"O Canada"

Notable Parties:
Kountry Kwencher, Highlighter

Drink of Choice:
Molson Light

Neighbors: AD

Gamma Delta Chi
Γ Δ X
"GDX"

It's true that the Gamma Delta Chi (GDX or Gamma Delt) used to hold rush BBQ's to keep from losing Math Club pledges to Sig Nu or MIT. And yes, it's true that among the purple haze induced, well, haze of the 70's a female or two may have been able to circumvent the strict "No Girls Can Join" clause in the GDX bylaws.

Today the brotherhood consists of primarily football and baseball players mostly as a result of Beta and Chi Gam being, respectively, officially and unofficially stripped of their ability to admit new members. GDX is famously home to "The Pit," a large basement to the basement that has romantic concrete floors, charmingly decorated pong tables, and is not up to fire code.

A fan of the house would tell you that GDX would be able to win a brawl against any other fraternity, win a pong game against a few fraternities, and win an IQ test against zero fraternities. Additionally, the ragers occurring after the baseball team wins an Ivy Championship, or the football team wins... a game, are a campus highlight.

A hater of the house would tell you that nobody cares because we go to an Ivy League school where nobody has ever been in a fight, anyway.

A normal person would tell that hater to shut the f*ck up because you can only wear hyphy flat brims with a dirty Phillips Exeter lax penny from '03 without getting your ass beat at an Ivy League school.

Parties: A-	Athletics: C-	Academics: C-

Heard at the pregame:
"Hooked on Fonix"

Notable Parties:
GDXmas

Drink of Choice:
Muscle Milk on the rox

Neighbors: Tri-Kap

Kappa Kappa Kappa
"Tri-Kap"

Tri-Kap boasts one of the largest, strongest, and most diverse brotherhoods on campus.* Tri-Kap brothers enjoy an incredibly close brotherhood and a strong tradition that has been intertwined with Dartmouth tradition since 1842.*

Tri-Kap formed out of a schism between members of a debating society that eventually led to the founding of Tri-Kap and Psi U. Tri-Kap has remained strong since 1842, with its current home at 1 Webster Ave. It is the oldest local fraternity in the country.

Tri-Kap is a staple of the Dartmouth Social Scene.* Two of Tri-Kap's most iconic events are Monday Night Freeze parties and massive dance parties the first Friday and big weekend Friday of every term. Tri-Kaps bring their passions to the house and the house gives brothers the tools and connections to grow as individuals at Dartmouth.*

Tri-Kaps can most likely be seen wearing iconic Green Tri-Kap shirts unfailingly during pledge term. Once pledges become brothers, Tri-Kaps can often be spotted wearing any number of sarcastic shirts commemorating big weekends, many of which have been passed down over the years from brother to brother. Because of Tri-Kap's letters, these shirts are sure to offend almost anybody outside of Hanover, although Tri-Kap was founded roughly twenty years before the Ku Klux Klan and never has or will had any connection to that despicable group.

*Citation needed

Parties: B-	Athletics: C-	Academics: A

Instrument of Choice:
Violin

Notable Parties:
Freeze, Dance Parties

Drink of Choice:
Sapporo

Neighbors: Tabard, GDX

Phi Delta Alpha
Φ "Phi Delt" Α

Founded in 1884 as the New Hampshire Alpha chapter of Phi Delta Theta national, Phi Delt fills the old-school/don't care niche at Dartmouth. The house became independent in 1960 over member eligibility issues, and has been known as Phi Delta Alpha ever since.

Based on the Massachusetts State pavillion from the 1896 World's Fair, Phi Delt's Corinthian columns tower over Webster Ave. Phi Delt blasts classic rock hits from the 60's, 70's, and sometimes even the 80's and 90's for all to hear, but you will never hear a Top 20 hit coming from the speakers. Parties often include live bands, but Phi Delt's most famous party, Reds, occurs on the first and last Monday of each term as students pack in past the point of safe fire code to fill up their red solo cups. While the brotherhood may not be as welcoming as your grandma, someone in the house will always be willing to play pong. Taking most of its membership from rugby and the Review, Phi Delt's are close-knit, sometimes insular, and always "don't care". While Animal House may have been written about AD, you can argue that the the Animal House mentality has moved to Phi Delt.

A fan of the house might say, "Its brothers are diamonds in the rough, and they have sick tunes coming from the porch."

A hater of the house might ask, "Why are there no girls here? It seriously looks like a grim version of the volleyball scene in Top Gun."

Brothers are most likely seen wearing a bequested sweatshirt with a hole in it or a Dartmouth Indian t-shirt.

| *Parties: B+* | *Athletics: B+* | *Academics: B+* |

Heard at the pregame:
"Ramble On" -Zeppelin

Notable Parties:
Reds, Block Party

Drink of Choice:
Batch

Neighbors: Chi Gam, Tabard

Psi Upsilon
"Psi U"

Founded in 1842, Psi U is the oldest fraternity at Dartmouth. Psi U is known for having a very tight brotherhood. This fraternity draws heavily from the rowing, skiing, swimming, sailing, and water polo teams and also has a large number of ex (high school)-athletes.

The physical plant is the oldest fraternity house on campus, built in 1907, and it's pretty clear that the architect failed to design it for 21st century frat life. Upon entering the basement, you will notice brothers playing pong and non-brothers struggling to adapt to Psi U's unique environmental conditions - loved by few and hated by many. The low ceilings make pong a different sport, while the poles in the second room can cause some infuriating bounces. Brothers hit a little lower here than at some other houses, which always annoys the purists. Psi U's are generally well-behaved and respectful around guests and girls, but things can get fratty late at night once the scene thins out.

A fan of this house might say, "Psi U balances a strong brotherhood with an active social scene. It's a fun place to hang out, especially if you're trying to have a big night."

A hater might say, "They're preppy assholes with an inflated sense of self-worth. Have fun working 100+ hour weeks on Wall Street. I hear AD is holding winter rush."

Most likely seen wearing: backwards hat, khakis, shit-kickers (Timberlands) in the winter/Sperry's in the spring.

Parties: B+	Athletics: B	Academics: B+

Heard at the pregame:
"Ants Marching"

Notable Parties:
Jack Wills

Drink of Choice:
Cr@wlers

Neighbors: Theta Delt

GREEK LIFE

Sigma Alpha Epsilon
Σ ᴀ "SAE" ᴇ

Sigma Alpha Epsilon is a national Fraternity founded in Alabama in 1856. You know what that means, right? That they're all gun-toting, seersucker-wearing, mint-julep-slurping douchebags? While this is still true of a sizable percentage of the brotherhood (seriously, if you don't like mint juleps you can go f*ck yourself), they have everything now: even Polish dudes. The brotherhood is a lively cross-section of campus: heavyweight rowers, lightweight rowers, swimmers, campus political whores, real-life political whores, and slacker stoners, and alcoholics.

The house is unusually clean for a Dartmouth frat, and it's in a weird location all alone on the opposite side of Novack. Fun fact: it actually sits right at the end of the old frat row, before the College tore it up and built Novack (SAE still owns the land under Novack and charges the College rent for it).

The brothers are known alternately for their southern hospitality and for being way too into pong, sometimes to the detriment of non-beer-based social interaction. SAE is a surprisingly open and accepting brotherhood and you're guaranteed to have a good time when you stop by. And while they've progressed into the 21st Century in some ways, don't be surprised if you're greeted at the door by a belligerent, blacked-out bro clad in pastels and Sperrys.

Parties: B	Lawn Games: B+	Academics: A

Heard at the pregame:
"White Christmas"

Notable Parties:
Jungle Party, Champagne

Drink of Choice:
Mint Juleps, duh!

Neighbors: Novack, Church

Sigma Phi Epsilon
"Sig Ep"

Sigma Phi Epsilon recently got themselves shirts that were baby blue and had pink teddy bears on them. The text of the shirt says: "Sig Ep: Hard as F*ck." The terrific irony of the shirts makes them some of the best gear on campus. Sig Eps are not hard as f*ck. In fact, they are famously soft. The most salient manifestation of this softness is Sig Ep's complete lack of a traditional pledge term.

The Dartmouth fraternity Omicron Pi Sigma was formed in 1908 and has been part of the national Sigma Phi Epsilon since 1909, with one short stint as a local again in the 70's. The most famous alum is Dr. Seuss, who would be constantly impressed with how zany his fraternity has become... you know, if he were still alive. Which he isn't. Sig Ep got a nice new house in the spring of 2011, and the fact that the fraternity had no house for nine months didn't deter any of their rush standing. They consistently get the highest number of shakeouts of any fraternity, likely because of the unique experience they offer. Sig Ep's most notable brotherhood activity is its Balanced Man Program, which pushes the brothers of Sig Ep to better themselves in cognizant ways.

A hater of the house would say, "Sig Ep is just a bunch of soft Frisbee players looking for a place to play pong sometimes."

Sig Eps are most likely seen wearing zany Croo outfits and dyed hair, because 98.4% of Sig Eps apply to be on Croo.

Parties: B-	Intramurals: A-	Academics: B+

Heard at the pregame:
"Ruff Ryder's Anthem"

Notable Parties:
Foam Party

Drink of Choice:
O'Doul's

Neighbors: AXA, KDE

Sigma Nu
Σ "Sig Nu" N

Sigma Nu a.k.a. Sig Nu a.k.a. "The Noodle"... how to describe it best. Your first experience with Sig Nu will probably be in playing pong. This isn't because Sig Nu is known for their pong abilities (quite the opposite, in fact), but rather because the brothers are accommodating to freshmen who are looking for a quick game.

The brothers themselves come from a variety of different pools, such as Casual Thursday (an improv group), the Jack-O-Lantern (the campus' humor magazine), or the Dartmouth College Marching Band (the College's marching band). Brothers can be found on the third floor of the house, known as "High Street," getting, umm... well, let's say they're not getting "street". The house didn't used to be this way, though. It used to be the crew house. You'll know that it's changed if you talk to any old Sig Nu alum and ask him what house he was in: "Sig Nu, but it was different back then."

A fan of the current house might point to the many extracurricular involvements of the brothers, cite the friendly and open atmosphere of the basement and of parties, and even look at house GPA (nerds have to have high GPAs, right?).

A hater would... yeah, a hater would call them nerds and say that Ultimate Frisbee is not a sport.

Sig Nu brothers are most likely seen wearing "Keggy the Keg" t-shirts that they bought freshman year and still think are awesome.

| Parties: NR | (M)Athletics: A | Academics: A- |

Heard at the pregame:
"Dartmouth Alma Mater"

Notable Parties:
80's Party

Videogame of Choice:
W.o.W.

Neighbors: BG

Theta Delta Chi
"Theta Delt"

Theta Delta Chi (also "TDX," or "Theta Delt") is affectionately known as "The Boom Boom Lodge" because a brother was shot twice after stealing a bottle of whiskey during prohibition. To this day the fraternity condones stealing alcohol, but frowns upon violence.

The brotherhood consists mostly of athletes. A storied track record of these athletes quitting their teams has prompted some to call TDX "a place where athletes go to die." But it's actually a place where athletes go to drink, experiment with drugs, and THEN decide if they want to continue waking up for 6 a.m. workouts four days a week.

TDX parties are so outrageous that S&S sometimes walks through unprompted to make sure everybody is alright. Also, the pong is some of the most athletic you will see at Dartmouth, AND the brothers have the highest adjusted GPA of any fraternity... as long as you adjust for having the best basement music and being awesome all the time.

A fan of the house would say, "TDX's are thoughtful, chivalrous, and some of the most accomplished gentlemen on campus."

A hater would mention, "TDX's think mostly about themselves, rarely let girls play pong, and occasionally struggle to achieve erection because they have had too much to drink."

A TDX would tell you to f*ck off if you asked what he thought about the brotherhood – he obviously doesn't have time for your insignificant little questions.

| Parties: A | Athletics: A- | Academics: B- |

Heard in their own heads:
"We tha Shit" -Young Jeezy

Notable Parties:
Pig Roast, 80's Party, TDXmas

Drink of Choice:
Keg of Bud Heavy

Neighbors: Psi U, Sig Delt

Zeta Psi
"Zete"

When Beta and Zete came back in '08 and '09 respectively, there was a big hubbub on campus. Both frats did some pretty messed up stuff to get derecognized. Zete went bye-bye for a few years, operating as an independent fraternity from '01 to '07, and then completely shuttering its doors and going dark from '07 to '09. Feminists protested its return, and alums pushed for a solid new rush class. Everybody wondered whether Zete would be able to overcome the same tough obstacles that Beta did and establish itself with a solid new identity and a great group of guys. We're still kind of waiting for that one to work itself out.

Zete works hard for rush and is getting steadily better classes, but is still struggling from going dark for those years and losing its connection to the past. On the upside, the alums and the college poured a shitload of money into the building, and it's nicer than most hotels now. Also, due to the fact that the bros here haven't had the time to get overdeveloped egos, Zete tends to be a pretty inviting place. You can recognize Zete pledges around campus because they are always carrying an empty bottle of laundry detergent. Nobody's sure what that's about.

According to alums, Zete was an Ultimate Frisbee house before it got derecognized. It's starting to return to that state, with many guys choosing to rush both Sig Ep and Zete. Don't ask those guys which their first choice is, though, otherwise things could get really awkward.

Parties: NR	*Athletics:* NR	*Academics:* A-

Neighbors: Beta, BG

Heard at the pregame:

"Last Resort" -Papa Roach

"Guess Who's Back?" -Eminem

Heard at the Party:

"Crickets" -Mother Nature

There's More!

Alpha Phi Alpha (APA)

APA is the nation's largest predominantly African-American fraternity. The Dartmouth Chapter shares the same goals as the National Chapter. Although mysterious and secretive in nature, when these guys party... they come out with a bang.

APA houses many varsity athletes, social pioneers, and all around good guys. It also is not confined to African-American membership, housing brothers of Latino, Native American, Caucasian, and Asian ethnicities.

Lambda Upsilon Lamda (LUL)

Lambda Upsilon Lamda, or "La Unidad Latina," stands as one of Dartmouth's premier organizations for Latino students on campus. It exists for the betterment of Latinos not only at Dartmouth, but in higher education in general. The fraternity's community service record is polished to say the least.

The brotherhood is actually pretty small, so strength in numbers certainly can't apply here. We think the members would agree with us when we say the strength lies in the quality of the brotherhood and their contributions on and off campus. If you here the phrases "UPSI" followed by "ILON" in close succession, you know you are in close proximity to members of this organization. They are known more for their intellectual strength rather than their parties, although I met one member who mixes a mean margarita.

Dartmouth
Sororities

"Do you ever wake up and wonder if you joined the right sorority? We sure do."

GREEN Editors

Understanding This Section

If you're a female reading this, you probably just forced a deep breath as you flipped to the sorority section. Who wouldn't when three male editors begin discussing the groups of girls inhabiting a campus? But we promise, you can relax.

All following sections have either been written or read by females that are in some way tied to the sorority system on campus.

To further calm your nerves, know that none of our female friends had a problem with the following sorority summaries (and if we do say so ourselves, that's a substantial poll).

That said, the following descriptions are to provide insight into each sorority as an individual house full of traditions and the girls you may find there. As the following pages will imply, though the rush process may be pretty flawed, the houses and communities it generates do have their charm.

Sorority Recruitment
Demystifying a mystified process

Sorority rush is an exciting time in a young Dartmouth girl's life. Like a tadpole ready to transform into a frog, sorority rush transforms anonymous schmobs of freshmen girls into readily identifiable (read: stereotypable) masses of, umm, friends.

For most of these young newts, their first knowledge of sororities and their sisters revolves around judging spring t-shirt colors, catchy slogans (Get PHIsyical!! psyKDElic <3), and the girls who mean-mugged them when they accidentally crashed their tails at Chi Gam after their totally cute, but clueless, trip leader said they should DEF come over early and drink. Idiot.

Pre-rush season starts off early spring with a series of PanHell-mandated organized events at each house. Depending on the house, these consist of a scrambedly assembled array of junk food, soda, and sisters to Stinson's BBQs and ice cream socials. **They make little to no difference in familiarizing you with each sorority since, for the most part, you go to the houses you've already stereotyped**, I mean, know and with sisters you've already judged, erm, know. While not as revealing of each house's personality as, say, playing Black Forest or attending Whipstock (the substance-improved fraternity equivalents of rush, for the un-informed), how little girls pre-rush matters is great: no worrying all the bros are going to ding you or have already named you "boner" on the account of that slight mashap when you excitedly hugged your partner after winning Harbor.

The **excitement is palpable when it comes time to rush**. After last ditch efforts to "get lunch" with that KDE who was a trip leader in their section or "hang out at Theta Delt" with that Kappa whose boyfriend they totally unknowingly hooked up with freshman spring, rush begins in clearly the most logical way to seal your social fate at Dartmouth. Haha. Kidding. Um, but just as we've handed our souls, social lives and soon-to-be arthritic fingers to smart phones, Facebook, and live tweeting, now we hand ourselves over the most awe-inspiring, powerful and demonstrative technology of them all: **the PanHell Mathematical Derivative for the Institution of Social Stereotypes 2.0 Beta. (PmDISS2.0)**

This all-knowing, all-seeing machine divides the girls from the gals, the Theta Delt biddies from the BG girls, and generally your group of freshmen friends. More literally, it divides you into "Rho Chi" groups of

"PNM's" (couldn't tell you what it stands for except that it's suspiciously close to "PMS"). If you're lucky (a.k.a. sign up for rush at the same time as your friends), you'll end up in a group with your biddies. If you're strategic, you won't.

The first two days of rush you'll spend going to each house with this group, occupying your time guessing what house your Rho Chi (a.k.a. the sorority sister who had the common sense to get out of rush by being an "advisor" to rushees) is in and gossiping excitedly about what house had the best outfits (80's prom! Arabian Nights!). **It's the best afternoon of overly caffeinated and sugared girl flirt you never thought you'd have.** Yes, a SERIOUS and SHOCKING statement here: rush parties are ACTUALLY FUN.

Anyway, on a full rush of adrenaline and eagerness, you'll rank the houses and through a top secret complex operation by PmDISS2.0, you'll find yourself invited back to four houses. These parties are more "personal," as topics move from your hometown, your favorite kind of cupcake and the interesting fact you picked to tell people about yourselves so you **don't come off as that generic girl who only talks about her major and what dorm she lives in** to the far more consequential topics of your thoughts on Drew Barrymore, gender relations on campus, and the time you were sent to the hospital with salamenella.

PmDISS2.0 makes another appearance to invite you to bid night: yes, systematically based on your answers to the aforementioned questions, your Facebook profile, and potentially your tweets, **this miraculous machine knows exactly what two houses would be the right ones for you.** In your honor, these houses perform cultic rituals that I would describe further, but well, I'd have to kill you. The house that scares you the least (or the one you've been determined to join since freshman fall) is usually the one you pick and live happily ever after!!! Haha. As if. Obviously the machine picks for you.

-Lia Grigg, Certified PanHellenic Analyst (C.P.A.), Class of 2011

Alpha Xi Delta
"AZD"

The Theta Psi chapter of Alpha Xi Delta ("AZD") was founded as Delta Pi Omega in 1997. Alpha Xi Delta initially occupied the house currently home to Beta Theta Pi, until Beta repossessed their house in 2008. In the fall of 2009, they moved into a newly renovated house at 17 East Wheelock Street.

Sisters can be seen wearing a ton of AZD gear around campus. Don't be surprised to see them hanging out in Collis every Wednesday, wearing their letters, and chatting over lunch. AZD is known for its event Karaoke for a Cause, which supports their national philanthropy, "Autism Speaks". They strive to create campus dialogue around autism awareness.

AZD's are DOC trip leaders, campus tour guides, varsity athletes, health education peer advisors, DREAM mentors, UGA's, tutors, sustainability advocates, TA's, musicians, artists, dancers, and true leaders on the Dartmouth campus. Their wide range of campus involvement makes them hard to pin down as a stereotype, and they have successfully eluded it for some time.

Academically, AZD excels. Some say their location next to East Wheelock cluster may contribute to their success in the classroom. With the highest GPA on campus, their membership boasts Rhode Scholars, law graduates, salutatorians, and recipients of competitive national scholarships.

Heard at the pregame:
Chatting

Notable Events:
Karaoke For a Cause

Drink of Choice:
Brain Toniq

Neighbors: Heorot

Alpha Phi
"A-Phi"

Alpha Phi has a close-knit sisterhood who participates in events and is active on campus and the community. They have sisterhood events such as apple picking and jewelry studio workshops every term and hold weekly chapter meetings and sisterhood dinners. And they can't wait to move into their new house! Construction will begin in the fall of 2011, and sisters will be able to move in in the fall of 2012. Until then, Alpha Phi occupies the 4th floor of Hitchcock dormitory.

The Alpha Phis at Dartmouth love **PHI-lanthropy.** They host events to raise awareness and funds for women's heart health, including an annual Red Dress Gala at the Hanover Inn and "Heart Health Week" during winter term. Other philanthropy Alpha Phis at Dartmouth take part in include: volunteering at CHAD, David's House, Relay for Life, local walks (ex: MS walk), the Prouty and other events on campus.

Alpha Phis are also involved in a number of other activities in the Dartmouth and Hanover communities, including: a cappella groups, Link-Up, dance groups, MAVs, EDPAs, DAPAs, tour guiding, club sports, and Women in Business. Also, they have members on the Panhellenic executive board, Programming Board, Hillel, Habbad, Aquinas House, Dartmouth Wind Symphony, Dartmouth Law Journal, DREAM, Big Brother/Big Sister, and LEAD to name a few. Many of their members are also Dartmouth athletes and play on the varsity basketball, volleyball, track and field, hockey, tennis, swimming, and equestrian teams.

Neighbors: Blunt Alumni Center

Heard at the pregame:
"I Got a PHI-lin'"

Notable Events:
PHI-estas!

Drink of Choice:
Gatorade PHI-erce

GREEK LIFE

Delta Delta Delta
△"Tri-Delt"△

Wake and bake with a Tridelt! Actually, marijuana has no relation to Tridelt. I just use the phrase because it would be a pleasure to wake up next to one and the "stereotype" for the house is that they bake things often, e.g. cookies and brownies. The girls also tend to be very attractive and down to earth, as the sorority is in the fabled "Top Three". They do quite well at rush.

Delta Delta Delta was founded in 1984, and as a national sorority, it isn't able to throw parties but still hosts many performance groups in fun, campus-wide events. Tridelts put their baking prowess to good use by having bakesale fundraisers in the library seemingly every other night. During Green Key, they also hold an annual pankcake brunch in order to raise money for their national philanthropic partner, St. Jude's Children's Research hospital.

Don't dare mention the word "Housewife" in conversation with a Tridelt, though. They're aware of the stereotype and distance themselves from it. They're leaders of many organizations on campus, top players on sports teams, and continually rank in the top two for highest Greek House GPA.

A hater of Tridelt would question whether the collective personality of the house could fit in at a mime convention, but those haters have obviously never joked around with a Tridelt when buying one of her baked goods. And come to think of it, mimes are strange.

A Tridelt is probably most often seen wearing some nice clothing.

Heard at the pregame:
"Up, Up, and Away" -Kid Cudi

Notable Events:
DHop, Novack Bake Sale

Drink of Choice:
One glass (max) of red wine

Neighbors: EKT, AXA

Epsilon Kappa Theta
"EKT"

Epsilon Kappa Theta was originally founded in 1982 as the 100th colony of the national sorority Kappa Alpha Theta (Epsilon Kappa chapter). The members decided to split from Kappa Alpha Theta in 1992 after tension between national rules and the chapter's values. The decision to go local is celebrated every May 4th, and the sisterhood will welcome Theta alumnae back for a special 20th birthday celebration in Spring 2012. The distinctive spires of Theta's physical plant can be found at 15 Webster Avenue, opposite the President's House.

Theta's members span campus in their interests, passions and creative outlets. The diversity of the organization's membership is a great source of pride for its members.

The sorority's philanthropic efforts are focused on directly impacting the local community. Sisters participate in regular fundraisers for WISE (an Upper Valley resource center which provides services to victims/survivors of sexual violence, domestic violence and stalking).

Thetas are best known for their strong sense of sisterhood. Members enjoy time together spent apple picking, road tripping to Montreal, making pottery, riding roller coasters at Six Flags and baking cake-balls (a secret Theta recipe).

The house also hosts two open parties each term. Graffiti Party gives attendees a chance to decorate each other's white t-shirts with colored markers. Later in the term is Thetaroo, a live-music event featuring student bands.

Heard at the pregame:
Loud Noisssess

Notable Parties:
Thetaroo

Drink of Choice:
Something Made in a Cauldron

Neighbors: Tri-Delt, AXA

Kappa Delta

"KD"

Kappa Delt goes by KD, pronounced "kay-dee". KD's national philanthropies are Girls Scouts and Prevent Child Abuse America. KD held its first annual Shamrock 5K this spring to benefit Prevent Child Abuse America and New Hampshire Children's Trust.

KD came to Dartmouth in the Summer of 2009 and has grown to 100 members as of Winter 2011. KD hosts its meetings in Tom Dent Cabin. Right now its physical plant is in Smith, but an actual house is coming very soon! KD's colors are olive green and pearl white. The sisterhood is part of a larger and very strong national sorority with over 250,000 members nationwide.

In case you were wondering, KD's national headquarters are located at 3205 Players Lane, Memphis, TN. Leanne Touhy, the inspiration of *The Blind Side,* is a Kappa Delta.

Neighbors: The River, Norwich, VT

Heard at the pregame:
The Blind Side Soundtrack

Notable Parties:
Tackis, Drby

Drink of Choice:
Br

Kappa Delta Epsilon
"KDE"

KDE is pronounced like KD, but with an "eee" at the end. "Zany" is the first word that comes to mind when one imagines a KDE. Then "empowered". Then "bold". Then "feminist". A lot of buzzwords come to mind, but they aren't actually representative of most of the sisterhood. In reality, the sum and the parts of this sorority are very different. The parts are a bunch of very awesome, cool girls.

The house has good diversity, and its sisters are held in high regard. It is also the most prominent local sorority on campus, founded in 1993. It has been steadily on the popularity rise since then and is now at the top of the social scene. Due to its local status and popularity, it is able to host a number of well-attended and fun parties.

A lot of KDE's take KDE really seriously, and this manifests itself best at the sorority's annual Derby party, held on the day of the Kentucky Derby and featuring appropriately chotchy garb. The hosts of the party enforce rules strictly, and don't even try to come without an invitation card! If you're in, however, it's one of the spring's best events.

A hater of the house would say that the zaniness can be obnoxious and that the reactionary feminism of the collective sisterhood could halt Hillary Clinton in her tracks.

They're most likely seen wearing Tackies, a pseudo-unattractive blend of loud clothing that they wear often for house events.

Neighbors: Sig Ep, Chigam

Heard at the pregame:
"It's All Coming Back to Me Now"

Notable Parties:
Tackies, Derby

Drink of Choice:
UFO

Kappa Kappa Gamma
"Kappa"

It's a party in the KKG with Kappa. Girls pine to be in this house and wear the blue ribbons of Kappa pledge term in their hair with pride. Kappa was founded in 1978 and is the oldest national at Dartmouth. Their kozy physical plant can be found on 24 East Wheelock St., and blends in well with its local neighbors.

Kappa's love spelling words with the letter "K". For instance: karrot, kids, and Mortal Kombat. Some may describe Kappa as a kult and you'll see girls blossom into sassy kweens when they join Kappa. Kappas can often be found in and outside of Collis, the Green, and Alumni Gym. Overall, Kappas love to show house pride through their Kappa gear. To give you an idea of the kind of gear we're talking about, Kappa's rush t-shirt that they gave to all their new '13s is neon and says, "Went Kappa." Swag on swag.

Kappas come from all over the country and abroad, though New York City tends to have an impressive lock on the ranks of Kappas. Also, New York Senator Kirsten Gillibrand '88 was a Kappa, which is a nice nod for the house.

A hater of Kappa would use "sassy" as a euphemism, not as an actual description. Sometimes it can be a little much.

Kappas are most likely seen wearing the ridiculous house gear that they get, including "Kappa Krop Tops".

Heard at the pregame:
"Take the Money and Run" - SM Band

Notable Events:
Kappa Krush, EBA's Semi

Drink of Choice:
Cowboy Margs

Neighbors: Amarna

Sigma Delta
"Sigma Delt"

Sigma Delta was the first sorority at Dartmouth. Founded in 1977 as a chapter of the national sorority Sigma Kappa, the house went local in 1988 because of discomfort with the national's heavy emphasis on religion and the traditional role of women in their rituals. Today, Sigma Delt prides itself on being a house of "strong women". When asked what kind of women Sigma Delt looks for, sisters will tell you that "the sisters define the house, not the other way around," meaning the identity of their sisterhood is constantly in flux, and they don't seek to recruit any specific type of girl. Sisters are heavily involved in a vast spectrum of campus activities, with a consistent presence in DREAM, DOC Trips, peer advising and varsity athletics.

Their physical plant at 10 West Wheelock, located in close proximity to Collis, features a basement with the names of every sister carved on the walls, class-painted pong tables, and a kitchen that is probably not fit for human habitation. Since Sigma Delt is a local sorority, the sisters are able to have an open basement at all times, and you'll frequently find sisters downstairs dancing on the benches to the house song or closing out the night with "bra pong".

The house votes on a philanthropic cause each term on which to focus their service efforts; the most recent organization was Women for Women, which helps female survivors of war rebuild their lives.

Heard at the pregame:
"Little Secrets" - Passion Pit

Notable Parties:
Heaven/Hell, Last Chance

Drink of Choice:
Brass Monkey

Neighbors: Theta Delt

GREEK LIFE

There's More!

Alpha Kappa Alpha

The Xi Lambda Chapter of AKA recently returned to campus in 2008 after a brief hiatus. AKA is a national African-American sorority with about 10 members per class. They are known for their positive activism, holding events and symposiums to discuss issues of race, gender, and class. Their programming-activities-to-members ratio would shame most fraternities and sororities on campus, and they would definitely be the first to let you know (well... the second now).

Sigma Lambda Upsilon

Sigma Lambda Upsilon, or "Señoritas Latinas Unidas Sorority," exists as the equivalent of LUL in sorority form. The "Hermanas" (Spanish for "sister") are not only from the Hispanic culture, and are drawn from all corners of campus in order to embrace Sincerity, Loyalty, and Unity. They emphasize the empowerment of underrepresented populations, community service and academic excellence.

Coeducational Houses

Alpha Theta

Alpha Theta claims to be Dartmouth's premier coeducational fraternity on campus; we have no idea if this is true or not. We are certain that if you want to get wrecked in Halo, World of Warcraft, or The Sims, Alpha Theta is the place to go. Challenging the hosts of "Dartcon" in any sort of fantasy video game is the equivalent of digital seppuku. Besides Dartcon, one event you can't miss is their "Seven Deadly Sins Tails," which is mostly attended by gluttons (the drinking kind)....so we really don't get where the other six come into play.

Phi Tau

Like milk and cookies? Then you'll love "Milque and Cookies," Phi Tau's termly and most popular event. Phi Tau, located behind Kemeny Hall on North Main Street, lives by the motto "Unity in Diversity," and their brotherhood consists of just that indeed. Unlike most basements on campus, you can actually walk barefoot in theirs without contracting an infectious disease. Fun Fact: their eternal president, Katherine Fightow, holds the record for the longest reign as a member of the GLC.

The Tabard

The Tabard, formerly known as Sigma Chi, hold's the status of Dartmouth's premier liberal coeducational Greek house, as they place absolutely no bias on race, gender, or sexual orientation. You may recognize the name from the Chaucer saga... what was it again? Anyway, Tabard has this weird association with cosmic blue things, which can be seen as alternative, I guess. If you're looking for a weird time, and I mean that subjectively, stumble on in to their weekly Wednesday open meetings. If you happen to like what you see there, join! Tabard has a rolling rush process and no "pledge" term, which is frankly awesome. One thing Tabard prides itself on is its openness to LGBTQA population on campus, which comprises some of their membership. Also, highlights that every student must experience once at Dartmouth are Tabard's Lingerie and Disco Inferno parties, which are absolutely out of control.

Appendix

"So informational, it hurts!"

Theodor Suess Geisel, 1904

Acknowledgments
A list of GREEN's awesome contributors

The GREEN editors would like to extend a special thanks to all of the book's contributors. While the following list is not all-inclusive due to several national mandates, we would like to include these ghostwriters in our gracious thoughts - it is a shame the world will know not of your enviable talents. God Bless America.

Jamie Berk

Grace Best

Hana Bowers

Hannah Conant

Charlie Dameron

Kevin De Regt

Tim Dolan

Hunter Dray

Eric Durrell

Steve Elliot

Michael Fields

Meredith Greenberg

Michelle Greenberg

Lia Grigg

Mostafa Heddaya

Anna Hickmen

Shamus Hyland
Chris Jenny
John Katz
Jared Klee
Kelley Kugler
Ben Ludlow
Tina Ma
Brendan Mahoney
Johnny Mathias
Jamie McLaughlin
Nick Pappas
Chris Parker
Jake Pruner
Alex Pujol
Fernando Rodriguez-Villa
Sidney Sands-Ramshaw
Carter Scott
Chris Silberman
Fiona Strawman
David Watson
Max Yoeli

A Dartmouth Glossary

@now – commonly used in emails, meaning "right this moment!"
'Shmob – Inevitable grouping of travelling freshmen looking to roll to a party
1902 Room – Where cracked out paper-writers go from 2 a.m. on into the night...
A-Lot – Where people park their car who are not in fraternities or sororities
Awk - Awkward
BEMA – "Big Empty Meeting Area": One of the Dartmouth Seven
Billy Bob – The Hop's marquee item: eggs, steak, and cheese (heart attack) in a wrap!
BlitzMail – RIP: Dartmouth's now defunct email system
BlitzJack - When someone sends an email from your account usually in a funny sense.
Boot - Vomit
Casper – Someone who flies under the radar socially but interests you in more ways than one
Crunchy – Term used to describe alternative environmentalists and tree-hugging outdoorsmen
DarTV – Crappy cable accessible via ethernet
DA$H – A debit account linked to your student ID
DBA – "Declining Balance Account": Your dining money that goes all too fast
DDS – "Dartmouth Dining Services": Where you spend your DBA
Dick's House – Dartmouth's infirmary/holding tank
Dimensions – Dartmouth's recruiting trip for non-athletes
Distribs – Categories of classes that are required to obtain credits for before graduation
DOC – "Dartmouth Outing Club" (see pg. 102)
Drill - Hell
Evolving Vox – Dartmouth's premier and best dorm furnishing company
Facetime – Act of soliciting attention by loitering in places where you are expected to loiter in (Novack, Collis Porch, FFB, TFB)
FFB – "First Floor Berry" i.e. facetime central
Flitz – Flirting over BlitzMail
Floorcest – Inter-floor (usually freshmen) hook-up action
FSP – "Foreign Study Program": Enables you to study a specific subject

in a foreign country
GDI – "God Damn Independent"
Gorf – Drain lining the basement of AD used for bodily fluid disposal
Gut – Class with little work, a high median, or an awesome prof
Hang Out – Going out or playing pong or drinking in general
Hanover FSP – Taking on off term and staying on campus
HB – "Hinman Box": Your Mailbox
Hop – The Hopkins Center for performing culinary arts
H-Po – The Hanover Police... steer clear!
Keggy – Dartmouth's unofficial mascot... in the shape of a keg
Ledyard Challenge – Swimming across the Connecticut... naked... the running back across the bridge into NH safe-haven
LNC – "Late Night Collis": Collis' buffet of food set out between 8 p.m. - 1 a.m.
LSA – "Language Study Abroad": A Dartmouth program that enables you to learn a foreign language native to the country in which you live.
Meetings – Semi-secret gatherings of fraternity and sorority members on Wednesdays
NAD – "Native American at Dartmouth"
NARP – "Non-Athlete-Regular-Person"
Nonner – Non-Athlete
NRO – "Non-Recording Option": You can choose to implement this and set a grade floor for the respective course you are in
Parkhursted – A(n) forced/enforced hiatus from Dartmouth campus as a result of breaking college rules
Polar Bear Swim – Winter Carnival activity of jumping into the frozen Occom Pond
Prospie – A potential Dartmouth student, most commonly used during Dimensions
Rage(y) – Party (party-like)
Rando – Semi-harsh term for a random person
Robo – Robinson Hall, houses the ski team locker-room sauna and the DOC
S&S – "Safety and Security": Campus Security
Self Call – Bragging about yourself
Swim Test – Do this. You have to.
Tackies – Garb worn by the sisters of KDE at their termly party
Townie – A resident of Hanover that has no association with this school
Trippee – Someone who was on the same Freshman DOC trip as you
UGA – Undergraduate Advisor: stationed on every dorm floor
X-Hour – An extra period a prof can choose to use (not use) once a week

Useful Phone Numbers

Dartmouth

Collis Center for Student Involvement: (603) 646-3399
Collis Information Desk: (603) 646-2100
Center for Women and Gender - (603) 646-3456
Computing Services - (603) 646-2643
Dartmouth Dining Services - (603) 646-2271
Department of Safety & Security:
(603) 646-4000 (non-emergency)
(603) 646-3333 (emergency)
East Wheelock Cluster - (603) 646-3376
Financial Aid Office: (603) 646-2451
Greek Letter Organizations & Societies - (603) 646-2399
Dick's House: Counseling/Mental Health Appointments - (603) 646-9442
Dick's House: Primary Care/Physical Health Appointments - (603) 646-9401
Hinman Post Office - (603) 646-2824
International Office - (603) 646-3474
Off-Campus Programs Office: (603) 646-1202
Office of the Dean of Undergraduate Students: (603) 646-2243
Office of Residential Life:
1. Undergraduate Housing: (603) 646-3093
2. Residential Operations: (603) 646-1203
3. Office of the Registrar: (603) 646-2246
4. Residential Education - (603) 646-1491
5. Student Accounts/Student Financial Services - (603) 646-3230
6. Student Life Office - (603) 646-2980

Food

Boloco - (603) 643-0202
Gusanoz - (603) 643-3003
EBA's - (603) 643-6135
The Orient - 603 643-8888
C&A's - (603) 643-2966
Mai Thai - (603) 643-9980

Ramunto's - (603) 643-9500
Yama - (603) 643-4000
Molly's - (603) 643-2570
Murphy's - 603-643-4121
Canoe Club - (603) 643-9660
Dirt Cowboy - (603) 643-1323
Subway - (603) 643-0360
Salt Hill - (603) 676-7855
Bagel Basement - (603) 643-2245
Lou's - (603) 643-3321

Misc.

Co-Op - (603) 643-2667
True Value - (603) 643-2308
CVS - (603) 643-3178
Norwich Wines and Spirits – (802) 649-1970
Gap - (603) 643-6733
Talbot's – (603) 643-1600
The Nugget – (603) 643-2769
Makin' Waves - (603) 643-1244
Walt and Ernie's – No appointment needed!
Ivy League Cuts and Tans - (603) 653-0067

The End

Thanks for reading, folks.

Made in the USA
Charleston, SC
25 July 2011